# NORTH WOODS

# NORTH WOODS

## An Inside Look at the Nature of Forests in the Northeast

*Peter J. Marchand*

APPALACHIAN MOUNTAIN CLUB
*Boston, Massachusetts*

NORTH WOODS
*AN INSIDE LOOK AT THE NATURE OF FORESTS IN THE NORTHEAST*
by Peter J. Marchand


Book design: Dede Cummings/Irving Perkins Associates, Inc.
Illustrations: Carol Stephens, David Cooper
Photographs: Peter Marchand
Composition: Graphic Composition, Inc.

ISBN: 0-910146-64-0
5 4 3 2 1 87 88 89 90 91

*To you, the reader, who care enough*
*to learn, and in whose understanding*
*rests the future of the North Woods.*

# CONTENTS

# PREFACE

ONCE IN A while a minor event triggers an idea that just won't go away. Sometimes you're not even aware of its happening, but like a tiny spore carried in the wind, such an isolated experience can survive and grow when it lights in the right place. The idea for this book sprang from such an innocent occurrence—a brief encounter with a group of strangers who stumbled into and out of my life in the space of just a few hours, and whose names and destination I never learned.

At the time, I was lying on the ground on a windswept ridge of Mount Lafayette in New Hampshire, scratching intently in the soil for signs of germinating seeds. I was hoping to learn something about the natural recovery of vegetation in a rigorous and limiting environment that was being loved to death by a burgeoning number of mountain enthusiasts. It was getting late in the afternoon, and one more straggling group of hikers—probably the last of the day—was plodding toward me on heavy feet. As they came within a few yards of my study site they stopped, although I'm sure they hadn't noticed me yet, and in the golden late-afternoon light one of them caught sight of the subtle but clear trace of old logging trails to the east on the flanks of Guyot. Yellow and paper birch had grown up in the strip of light opened by the skid trails and now, in thin lines of a different green, ran in slightly diagonal, evenly spaced tiers to the highest ridge tops and across nearly every mountain to the south and east of the Pemigewasset Wilderness. The hikers were struck by these lines but perplexed by their cause. I eavesdropped on the conversation that followed with delight, impressed by the hikers' initial observations and fascinated by the debate that ensued.

Later that evening we all ended up in Greenleaf Hut, at the treeline on Mount Lafayette, and as inevitably happens, we got to talking about the range and its natural history. I had spent countless evenings at the hut in similar conversation, but this time was different. The discussion was truly electric, sparked by a curiosity that seemed boundless. We talked about those logging trails, about the "blowdowns" crossing the trail down to the hut (my companions had never heard of fir waves, a topic I'll discuss in Chapter III), about the bog forming at the end of Eagle Lake, and about the clouds building and dissipating over North Peak. On and on we went—and I guess it was then that I decided, quite unconsciously, to try this book.

What I had in mind from the beginning was a guide to the ecology of northern forests and alpine tundra in the northeastern United States. A number of excellent field books were already available and could assist in the identification of just about anything living, but I wanted to deal more with the *hows* of landscape development and with the functional relationships between organisms and their environment. Of course, executing this ambition

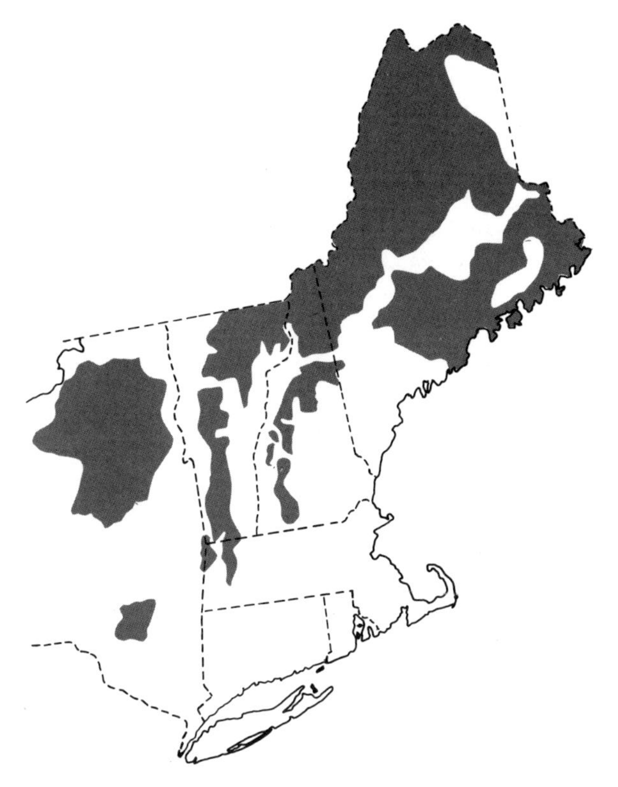

*Distribution of spruce-fir and northern hardwood-spruce forests in the Northeast United States. (Based on A. W. Küchler,* Potential Natural Vegetation of the United States, *American Association of Geographers, 1964.)*

turned out to be far more difficult than I imagined, and what I ended up with was a little of both approaches. In general I have remained faithful to my initial goals, but it is difficult to talk about bog succession without showing what a few heath shrubs look like, or to discuss the distribution of spruces without illustrating the difference between a red spruce and a white spruce. So I have described some of the more common plants of the North Woods, but mostly I have limited myself to helpful hints for identifying trees while you are exploring backroads at 30 miles per hour, when you are laboring with a heavy pack on the trail and can't look up, or when the tree you want to know is on the opposite bank of the river. This book is not intended to be a substitute for a good field identification manual. Rather it should be used in conjunction with books like Fred Steele's *At Timberline*, Lawrence Bliss's *Alpine Zone of the Presidential Range*, the Appalachian Mountain Club's *Guide to the Mountain Flowers of New England*, or any of several other good field guides.

I have written this book with northern New England and the Adirondacks in mind—the region north of a line running roughly from Old Forge, New York, through Rutland, Vermont, to Portland, Maine, and encompassing the High Peaks of the Adirondacks, the northern Green Mountains, and the White Mountains of New Hampshire and Maine. However, the book's usefulness is by no means restricted to this area, for outside of this region lie many pockets of northern hardwood and spruce-fir forest, such as the Mount Monadnock region of southern New Hampshire, Mount Greylock and the surrounding Berkshire Hills in Massachusetts, and the Catskills in southern New York State, all shown on the accompanying map. And of course to our north lies a great expanse of forest in Quebec and the Maritime Provinces for which this book is appropriate too.

Like the geographic area that it covers, *North Woods* is something of a mixed bag, a selective odyssey touching on aspects of forest, bog, and alpine ecology that have always interested me and perhaps have caught your own attention. To those of you who share with me a special feeling about these environments, who like nothing better than to hike the mountain trails or canoe the backwaters of the spruce-fir country or maybe just wander around on unpaved roads in an evening, and whose curiosity will never be fully satisfied, I hope this book helps a little.

*Peter J. Marchand*
*Johnson, Vermont*

I.

# *Reading the Landscape:* The Influence of Nature and Human Culture on a Forested Countryside

## *Emergence from an Ice Age*

JUST TWELVE THOUSAND years ago, the last great continental ice sheet pulled back from the mountains of northern New England and New York State to reveal a wholly remolded landscape. Gone were the craggy peaks and ridges of the eroding Appalachians; gone were the sharply incised valleys of rivers still cutting their channels downward; and gone, too, were the forests that had previously flourished in the region. The summits were rounded now, worn down by moving ice a mile thick, and the river valleys had been scoured into wide troughs with smoothly concave sides, as huge tongues of ice had flowed and ebbed in these natural channels. The soils of the previous millennia had been carried away to the sea, and now the freshly pulverized rock debris strewn about the land was slowly being colonized by a few hardy pioneers of the plant world—a handful of arctic species that wintered the Ice Age at the glacier's southern edge. This was the beginning, the preparation of the ground that ultimately would support the Northeast's present forests and alpine tundra.

For perhaps two thousand years or so, the landscape, covered with a tundra vegetation dominated by sedges and dwarf shrubs, resembled the arctic of today. Barren-ground caribou and musk-oxen roamed throughout the area, as evidenced by remains found as far south as the continental shelf area off the Connecticut coast (when much of the earth's water was still tied up in glacial ice, many such shelf areas were dry arctic plains). Gradually, though, the climate warmed; the tundra mammals moved north, following the waning ice; and boreal forests of spruce and fir appeared on the land. Analysis of pollen grains in pond-bottom sediments and in the peat deposits of bogs shows that spruces were the earliest of the conifers to arrive. They first invaded the river valleys and then slowly made their way up the hillsides (*Figure 1*), outcompeting the tundra plants for space and resources as they spread. Fir trees soon followed and proved even more successful than the spruces, and it wasn't long before firs dominated the higher mountain slopes. As the evergreen forests encroached, the shrinking tundra was gradually crowded higher and higher, finally relegating the last remnants of an arctic landscape to the colder mountain summits and deep ravines where they persist even today. Meanwhile in the valleys, scattered broadleaf trees were appearing: first the more northern species—aspen, paper birch, and alders—and then, about nine thousand years ago, trees of warmer climates—oaks, ashes, and maples, accompanied by white pine and hemlock. The climate would oscillate a little, becoming warmer than the present for the next four to six thousand years, then cooling; and the relative abundance of these species would shrink and swell accordingly. But eventually, a scant two thousand years ago, the northern hardwoods association dominated by American beech, sugar maple, and yellow birch became established locally throughout the region. And along with the hardwoods,

FIGURE 1 *Uplands of the North Country ten thousand years ago? This photograph was taken recently from a helicopter over interior Alaska, but it might just as well have been taken in the Northeast shortly after the region's last glacial episode. For about two thousand years after the retreat of the continental ice sheet from the Northeast, tundra vegetation dominated the landscape. With gradual climatic warming, however, spruce and fir slowly made their way northward from their own Ice Age retreat, advancing into the more protected river valleys. From there they progressed slowly up the hillsides, gradually displacing the tundra plants and animals, until a new balance was reached between climate and vegetation. The present zonation of forest and tundra in the northern Appalachians reflects this history of change and of present climatic influence on plant growth.*

spruce, for some unknown reason, regained prominence on the middle slopes.

So time, succession, and the domineering forces of climate all played their part in the greening of this freshly glaciated landscape. Through time, the elements worked to break down old rock into new soil material, releasing nutrients to the young vegetation cover. Succession then brought one plant community after another in steady progression, altering the growing conditions of a site, contributing organic matter to the soil, and recycling nutrients before they were lost downstream. The local climate controlled chemical and biological reaction rates and ultimately mediated the balance of competition between one species and another. Thus did the Northeast's present forests begin to take shape.

Eventually the European settlers of this region would have their impact on the forests too—something we will discuss in more detail shortly. But long before they arrived, the roots were down, and through all the changes that humans have wrought, the region's woodlands have retained their distinctly boreal character, a legacy of glaciers past and climate present.

## *When the North Winds Blow*

MANY FACTORS CONTRIBUTE to the boreal aspect of the North Woods landscape, but none is more important in maintaining this character than the regional climate, for it controls so many other physical and biological processes that govern the development and organization of plant communities. The climate of this region is, in fact, something of an anomaly: it is said that nowhere else at the same latitude in the northern hemisphere is it as cold as in the Northeast, except perhaps in northeastern China and Hokkaido, Japan. Old Forge, New York, and Portland, Maine, are situated at the same latitude as the French Riviera but share very few features, climatically or otherwise, with the palm-lined Côte d'Azur. Instead, average lowland temperatures in the Adirondack–northern New England region approach those of Anchorage and Helsinki, locations 15 degrees in latitude (almost a thousand miles) farther north. And the weather is still worse in the mountains. Consider that in the White

Mountains the treeline barely reaches 4500 feet above sea level, which makes it one of the lowest anywhere in the world at its latitude. It is often said that the summit of Mount Washington in New Hampshire has the world's worst weather—a subjective judgment certainly, but where hurricane-force winds and subfreezing temperatures can occur in any month of the year, who would argue?

The obvious question then, is what circumstances create this unusual climatic situation? The answer lies partly in the pattern of atmospheric circulation in the northern hemisphere. Low-pressure systems, whether developing in the tropics or elsewhere, converge on New England like migrating geese on a corn field. In fact, on a map of North American storm tracks (*Figure 2*), New England looks like a major freight yard where lines from the South Atlantic, the Gulf region, and even the Pacific Northwest all merge, tending to follow the northern coastline or to move up the St. Lawrence Valley. By itself, this steady progression of transient lows makes for interesting weather changes, but another phenomenon adds to the activity. Because the flow of air around a low-pressure system is counterclockwise, the backside of a low moving out of the St. Lawrence Valley or up the coast of Maine always brings with it winds from the north (see *Figure 3*). And these winds are often reinforced by the clockwise circulation of high-pressure cells that develop over the Hudson Bay region. By this circulation pattern, then, every low-pressure system passing over the Northeast tends to drag cold Canadian air in behind it, subjecting the region to frequent intrusions of polar air year-round. This repeating scenario goes a long way toward explaining the Northeast's unusually cool climate.

To this alternating progression of high- and low-pressure cells is added an elevational effect that greatly amplifies weather conditions. The mountain ranges in

FIGURE 2 *An analysis of 1160 storm tracks across the United States during a ten-year period shows how low-pressure centers converge over the Northeast. The width of the arrows on this map indicate the relative frequency of storms traveling a given path. This convergence explains in large part the weather patterns that make the Northeast's climate somewhat anomalous for the region's latitude. (Map from Van Cleef, 1908,* Monthly Weather Review, *U.S. Department of Agriculture, 36:56–58.)*

the area obstruct the path of moving air, like boulders in a rushing stream, and any air mass swept along in the general circulation of the earth's atmosphere must rise as it encounters these mountain barriers (see *Figure 4*). As it rises, the air cools as it expands under the decreasing atmospheric pressure of higher elevations. The air temperature falls an average of 3 degrees F for every 1000 feet gained but may drop as much as 5 degrees F under cloudless conditions. And when a rising air mass laden with moisture cools below its condensation point (the

FIGURE 3 *Shifting winds of the North Country. Winds in the northern hemisphere circulate in a counterclockwise direction around low-pressure centers and clockwise around high-pressure centers. Notice in the illustration that the flow of air (short arrows) between high- and low-pressure systems in the Northeast is complementary. For this reason, each low-pressure system passing through the region via several major storm tracks (long arrows) tends to pull a high-pressure cell in behind it. This steady progression of lows and their following polar highs gives the Adirondack–northern New England region its characteristic weather patterns.*

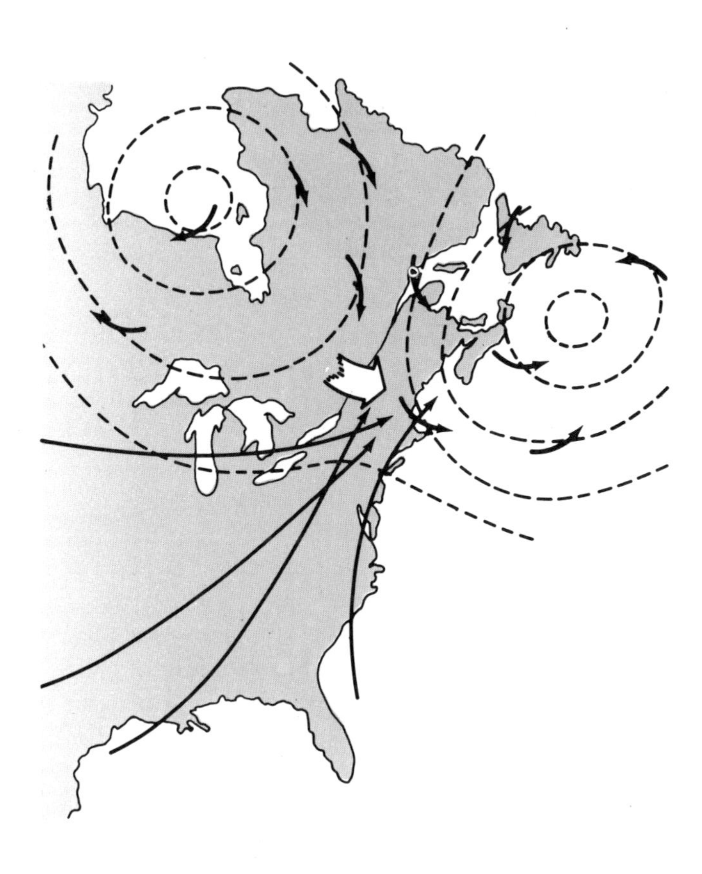

FIGURE 4 *Mountain weather maker. Moving air masses forced to rise over mountain barriers are often squeezed between the upper stable layers of the atmosphere and the mountain ridges and summits. This constriction creates a venturi effect; like a river funneled through a narrow gorge, the flow of air accelerates giving rise to the high winds typical of mountain slopes. As air ascends over the mountaintops, it also cools, and the effect of cooling is to wring moisture out of the mountain air. The effective precipitation at higher elevations increases still more as the forest canopy strains water droplets out of passing clouds.*

temperature at which it can no longer hold all the water vapor it contains), dense cloud cover forms over the mountains, often accompanied by rain or snow showers. It is not surprising, therefore, that the amount of precipitation collected at higher elevations in the Northeast is often double that measured at lowland stations and may reach as much as 80 inches annually. But as impressive as such measurements might be, they still underestimate the amount of moisture available to the high forests. Even when there is no measurable precipitation, the dense needle-leaf canopy of subalpine spruce and fir strains water from every cloud that sweeps across the mountain slope, leaving the forest dripping with cool moisture while the rain gauges remain empty.

The net result of this mountain effect is an unusually high frequency of cloud cover over much of the Northeast. To the surprise of many, the northernmost counties of Vermont and New Hampshire are as cloudy as the Olympic Peninsula in Washington, and this cloudiness, of course, contributes further to the North Country's comparatively low growing-season temperatures.

But the mountain effect doesn't end there. The aspect of a slope (the compass direction it faces) and its exposure to wind also affect the forest microclimate, the climate within and under the canopy of trees. A north-facing slope receives less solar radiation than a south-facing slope and thus tends to be cooler and somewhat wetter, usually supporting more conifers. Likewise, a slope exposed to higher winds will also have a cooler microclimate. A plant canopy absorbing sunlight usually heats up several degrees if the air around it is calm, but high winds dissipate that heat and thus deny the plants that slight thermal advantage. And when the growing season is short to begin with, slightly reduced temperatures can make a considerable difference in the nature of forest vegetation.

Although it seems almost a contradiction, valley floors in the hill country are cold spots too, but for a very different reason. At night, the ground loses heat through radiational cooling and chills the air, which thus becomes heavier and slowly drains downslope to collect in the bottomlands. On a clear, still night, when radiational cooling is at its greatest, an air-temperature difference of 15 to 20 degrees F can develop between a basin and an adjacent hillside just 400 feet or so higher. In such "frost pockets" the growing season is shorter still and the coldest temperatures of winter are recorded.

As a combined result of the atmosphere's general circulation pattern and the local topographic controls, only those plant species that are well adapted to cool, short growing seasons and at least occasional winter temperatures of –40 degrees F or lower are able to proliferate in the northern Appalachians. It is not surprising then, that much of the natural vegetation of northern New England and the Adirondack region represents a southward extension of Canada's vast boreal forest. Except for the presence of red spruce, whose distribution is largely limited to the northeastern United States, the makeup of our North Woods is much the same as throughout southern and central Quebec. Along the meandering stream flats of the colder bottomlands, where the often saturated soils are slow to release their nutrients, only the northern conifers can compete successfully for limited site resources. Often, too, these boreal outliers open up into treeless bogs of acidic peat and heath shrubs—a common sight in the glaciated region of eastern Canada. Elsewhere, on less extreme sites, the northern hardwoods dominate much of the landscape. As we will see shortly, the present expansiveness of hardwood forests in the northern Appalachians may be an artifact of past and present logging practices, but these trees, too, are well adapted to a cool climate, although they generally require better drainage and warmer, richer soils than the lowland conifers. Above 3000 feet in elevation the northern conifers again dominate the slopes, along with all the associated understory plants of the Canadian boreal forest. These communities, then, make up the Northeast's North Woods—quiet, enduring, almost mystical forests of gray mists, weathered trees, and sun-flecked, mossy-green floors.

## *Forest for the Taking*

OUR NORTH WOODS might resemble the vast coniferous forests of neighboring Canada even more closely were it not for the lasting influence of early land-use practices following European settlement of New England and the Adirondack region. Our understanding of the landscape before us cannot be complete without some sense of what has happened here in the last three hundred years.

When colonists landed in Massachusetts Bay in the early 1600s, they were surprised to find open, parklike woodlands with large tracts of land already cleared. This region was home to the Nipmuc, Pokanoket, and Narragansett tribes, whose agricultural practices and never-ending quest for firewood had pushed back the forests some distance from their settlements. In fact, so consuming was the native Americans' own need for wood that they apparently believed the European settlers had set sail for North America because they had run out of wood back home.

The colonists didn't have to venture too far inland, though, to reach old-growth forests of mixed hardwoods and conifers, with trees of a stature probably never before seen by these Europeans. In central New England they found white pine and hemlock growing 3 feet in diameter and 150 feet tall amid a diverse assemblage of southern broadleaf trees—oaks, hickories, and chestnuts—and the northern hardwoods—beech, maples, and birches. In the mountain regions, however, the colonists found forests of a different character, dominated by the northern conifers. Spruce and fir, it appears, were much more widespread then. And growing as they often do—very thickly, with a dense understory of saplings and a tendency to retain stiff, dead lower branches—they must have made progress very difficult for forest explorers; the earliest settlers of New England described the forests of northern Appalachians as "daunting terrible," "full of rocky hills as thick as molehills in a meadow, and clothed with infinite thick woods," "a wrath of savage vegetation."

Conditions changed quickly, however. By the early part of the eighteenth century, settlement of the New York–New England uplands was well underway and forests were falling rapidly to the colonists' bucksaws and axes. Land was being cleared for agricultural purposes, and what had seemed an inexhaustible supply of wood, generally treated as something to be gotten rid of as expediently as possible, was disappearing at an almost unbelievable rate. By the 1830s central New England was as much as 80 percent cleared and, ironically, wood had become so scarce around the major population centers that construction lumber had to be imported by ship from Maine and by rail from areas to the north and west; and only the introduction of coal into the cities averted a major fuel crisis. Even in the northern Green Mountains, early photographs show the land almost entirely cleared up to elevations of 2500 feet. Agriculture was flourishing in the North Country too, with sheep grazing the mainstay of many settlements.

The extension of railroads into northern New England and upstate New York put still more pressure on the area's remaining forests, as low-cost transportation and ready markets to the south spurred new commercial logging ventures. By 1850, lumbering operations had pushed from all directions into the heart of the Adirondack High Peaks region, and not thirty years later the forest products industry in northern New Hampshire had become one of the leading industries in that state. Pulpwood was in increasing demand, and in many areas clear-cutting was the harvest method of choice. By 1890 it was estimated that almost all softwood of commercial value had been removed from the White Mountains.

With the disappearance of the forests, the wildlife that once governed the economy of simpler lives vanished too. A number of factors were at work. The large carnivores—wolves, mountain lions, even the black bear—were bountied almost from the day the Europeans arrived, and extreme hunting pressure contributed to the demise of other game animals. But it was primarily the loss of forest habitat that led to the disappearance of so many species, and the list of victims was a long and often surprising one. In 1854, the prominent natural historian Zadock Thompson wrote in his *Natural History of Vermont* of the last known account, twelve years earlier, of a beaver in the state. And although it is hard to believe today, the white-tailed deer and wild turkey, which once sustained so many native Americans, were driven to extinction in these parts too; they were reintroduced by game managers only with the return of suitable forest habitat in the twentieth century.

What followed this episode of land clearing is an interesting chapter in the forest history of the Northeast and bears directly on what we see today. By 1850, the productivity of the northern hill farms had diminished considerably and many residents were giving second thought to farming. The industrial revolution was gaining momentum and promising a better living in the cities, the railroads had opened up the rich prairies of the Midwest, and word had come of gold in California. The lure of all this was great indeed—and then came the Civil War to pull still more young men away from the farm. Agriculture in the North Country had seen its brightest days; by the 1860s farms throughout the region were being abandoned on an unheard-of scale, and the pastures and croplands were simply left to revert back to forestland.

But the same forest type that we see today did not immediately reclaim the fallow land. In the warmer river valleys and lake basins, and in more southern parts, white pine was emerging as never before. The few old pines left scattered throughout the region had provided ample seed that, with its large store of food reserves, established itself well amid the highly competitive pasture grasses. White pine trees in dense stands soon dominated the old fields in warmer areas. In the colder hill country the farmlands were often reclaimed by the northern conifers—red and white spruce, balsam fir, white cedar—which encroached with less aggressiveness than the fast-growing white pine, but with the same result. In these neglected fields, where grass roots stubbornly held their ground, the conifers seemed to have a considerable advantage over the lighter, less drought-resistant seeds of the hardwoods.

Where white pine became established, the even-aged stands grew quickly, but because they could not reproduce in their own shade, the pines soon gave the understory over to the more shade-tolerant northern hardwoods. And in just fifty years the white pines were ready for harvest—a gift of nature to landowners who had invested only taxes on the abandoned acres. By the turn of the twentieth century, a new wave of clear-cutting had begun and another lumber boom was underway throughout the Northeast. From 1895 to 1925 an estimated 15 billion board feet of lumber, with a market value of $400 million, was logged off the central New England uplands alone.

In just three decades the white pine boom was over. The land once more was left to its own resources, only this time things were different. Instead of being covered with dense pasture grasses, the ground had been thoroughly scarified—the organic floor torn up by the skidding of logs and mineral soil exposed everywhere. And the hardwoods that had earlier established themselves under the pine overstory, and had been ignored by the loggers, were now heirs-apparent to the cleared sites. Before long their countless progeny sprang up from the bare mineral seedbeds. The face of the land was changing again; by 1930, northern hardwoods dominated throughout much of the region.

By the accounts of early foresters in the northern Appalachians, similar events had been altering the spruce-fir woods. Alfred Chittenden, a forest inspector for the U.S.D.A. Bureau of Forestry, wrote in 1905 that the forests of northern New Hampshire had been "primarily a spruce country but lumbering has brought about a great change in the species." This was echoed some years later by Marinus Westveld, a silviculturist with the U.S. Forest Service, who wrote that "by 1913 most of the owners in the Northeast were cutting their pulpwood lands clean. . . . Areas which had supported nearly pure stands of spruce and fir were left practically treeless. Elsewhere the hardwoods, not being generally utilized, dominated the residual stand and produced yearly vast quantities of seed, resulting in a greatly increased representation in the following crop." Today in much of the northern Appalachians we are looking at that "following crop"—expansive second-growth hardwood forests well suited to the climate and site conditions of the area, but maintained in their present state largely through the discretion of the wood-using industry (*Figure 5*).

FIGURE 5 *Clear-cutting of spruce and fir on better-drained lowland sites has led to the vigorous intrusion of hardwoods in many areas throughout the northern Appalachians. The conifers often seed back into the understory and might eventually reclaim the forest, but repeated selective cutting of these softwoods perpetuates the growth of hardwoods. In the pulpwood operation shown above, in northwestern Maine, all the conifers in the forest stand to the left are being harvested, leaving a mixed stand of birch and maple (below). Fifty years from now, the maturing northern hardwoods will look like a product of natural succession, as though they alone were the climax species on this site.*

## *Plant Succession: A Land in Transition*

THIS BRIEF REVIEW of the Northeast's forest history has already introduced the concept of succession and has described several sequences of change in vegetation following disturbance of one sort or another. It is time now to define succession in greater detail, for to understand the North Woods landscape of today requires more than just an appreciation of the land-use history and of how climate influences tree growth. Forests are dynamic, ever changing by their own forces; and the real key to interpreting the present-day distribution of forest communities lies in fully understanding the processes of forest succession.

*Succession* may be defined as the orderly replacement over time of one species or association of species (the community) by another, as a result of competitive interactions between them for limited site resources. Succession occurs because plant species themselves physically modify the site they occupy and do so in a way that shifts the balance of competition from one species to another, making possible the eventual invasion of a site by species that might not have been successful under initial site conditions. Using a simple example, here is how succession might work.

A newly exposed gravel bank is left by a waning glacier or shifting river, and within a short time species A becomes established on it. Species A has an advantage because it has nitrogen-fixing root nodules and therefore can obtain essential nitrogen from the atmosphere. Other non-nitrogen-fixing plants that arrive at the site find the soil too infertile and soon die out. With each succeeding generation, however, species A contributes organic nitrogen to the site, gradually increasing the fertility of the soil to the point where species B can successfully invade. Species B—a taller, faster-growing shrub, let's say—soon forms a dense canopy that intercepts much of the light that previously reached the soil surface. Species A, intolerant of shade, now gradually disappears, having been outcompeted by species B not for soil nutrients, but for available light. By its own success, species A had changed the site in such a way as to favor its competitor.

In time, another species appears, species C, which we'll say is a shade-tolerant conifer. Under the dense shrub cover in the moist organic soil created by the annual litterfall of species B, this newcomer marks time until a local disturbance, perhaps selective cutting by beavers, creates small openings in the shrub canopy. Species C responds to the increased light, grows quickly up through the openings, and eventually forms a new canopy. The acidic soil conditions created by this new dominant species render the site less suitable for species B, which gradually disappears. And so the process goes on.

This example represents what is sometimes called floristic relay succession. Not all succession works exactly as illustrated here, but such a model is appropriate for many of the forest communities around us. As described here, succession ends (or, rather, slows to an imperceptible rate of change until another disturbance occurs) when canopy dominance is attained by a species that is understory tolerant and, thus, able to reproduce in its own shade. This species or group of species is likely to be slow growing but long lived, a producer of less abundant but highly successful seed crops, and otherwise ideally suited to the particular habitat and able to hold the site against all invaders. The overstory species, along with their associated understory plants, comprise the climax community for a given site.

Typically, the role of pioneer, the early colonizer of a new or disturbed site, is played by only a few species that can tolerate the extremes of environment often characterizing a disturbed site. In northern parts, aspen, gray birch, paper birch, and pin cherry are the most common pioneers among the tree species. These species tend to be highly mobile and produce abundant seeds yearly—seeds that are adapted for efficient dispersal or long viability in the soil while awaiting an opportunity to germinate. Once established, these trees are fast growing and may completely dominate a site in the early going; but pioneer species are normally short lived and soon relinquish their ground to others.

These are only generalizations, however, and not all players follow the rules. Whether or not the pioneering tree species in a given situation are hardwoods or conifers often depends on previous land use. We have already seen that white pine is an important pioneer species in old-field succession in warmer areas of the northern Appalachian region. And where white pine does take over after disturbance or field abandonment, its tenure may be relatively long by virtue of its three-to-four-hundred-year life span. But its place is never permanent. As a closed canopy develops, the shade-intolerant pine is replaced in the understory by more tolerant species that eventually bring about a change in cover type. In northern areas, the role of old-field pioneer is sometimes taken over by conifers such as red or white spruce, which we normally think of as late successional species (*Figure 6*). When this occurs, much of the usual species progression is short-circuited and the initial community remains stable over time—essentially a climax community right from the start.

The greater ability of the conifers (as opposed to hardwoods) to invade abandoned pastures and hay fields may be related to their large, relatively heavy, wind-disseminated seeds, which can work down to the soil surface and provide enough stored energy to develop a

FIGURE 6 *This abandoned field in northern Vermont is being reclaimed quickly by red spruce, a shade-tolerant species that normally dominates in later stages of succession. In situations like this, the conifers are able to cope with the highly competitive grasses and often share the site with pioneering hardwoods, thus bypassing the usual order of species succession.*

seedling large enough to compete successfully with the grass cover. The natural drought resistance of these species also enables the seedling to withstand surface drying and severe root competition. But such ecological characteristics do not confer any particular advantage in invasion of sites where the mineral soil has been exposed. Whenever disturbance results in the removal of the sod or litter layer, the fast-growing, relatively shade-intolerant pioneer hardwoods are more likely to become established.

As succession proceeds from the early stages of colonization to the point of canopy closure by long-lived shade-tolerant trees, the internal organization within the forest steadily increases. Initially, only a relatively few plant species occupy the site, as the number of pioneers adapted to disturbed conditions is somewhat limited. With time, though, more and more species enter into the picture: species of narrower occupational specialization who partition space and resources ever more intricately in their bid to coexist. Plants with differing light requirements come to occupy different levels of the understory, while roots of differing architecture explore different levels of the soil. Mosses move into the pockets of deep shade, where they retain moisture better, while lichens move up to find light in the crowns of trees. Saprophytic fungi garner sustenance by processing dead plant material as it accumulates from above, while parasitic fungi find it easier to tap the already scant energy reserves of aging trees. And so the resources of the site are divided.

With increasing diversity of plants comes an increase in the numbers of animal species too, and the pathways of energy flow in the forest community become still more complex. Meadow voles and jumping mice may dominate the small grassy openings in the early stages of succession, but as the nature of the forest floor changes over time, so does the faunal competition. Accumulating litter and deadfalls provide cover for animals of other occupations. Deer mice harvest the fungi that have become so abundant, and in the decaying duff, spiders explore for small insects and fall prey themselves to the hungry short-tailed shrew. The nocturnal flying squirrels move into the rotted-out branch of the old yellow birch and divide feeding time with the red squirrels who run the day shift. And presiding over all are the larger carnivores and winged raptors, while the decomposers—the bacteria, fungi, and invertebrates of the forest floor—have the last word.

Thus the food web branches out and the internal circles of nutrient transfer grow ever wider as forest succession proceeds. The maturing forest is much more than just the sum of its individual parts, an odd assort-

### UNDERSTORY TOLERANCE AND FOREST SUCCESSION

*The tolerance of tree seedlings to understory conditions is not a characteristic that lends itself to precise measurement, yet common experience tells us that certain species consistently reproduce successfully in the shade of an overhead canopy, while others almost never do. Knowledge of how one species fares relative to another in this regard proves extremely useful in understanding the successional status of a forest stand: how it came to be what it is and where it is headed in the future. The following table indicates the relative understory tolerance of the most common tree species in the North Woods:*

#### TOLERANT

Able to survive in deep shade, the following species characterize the North Woods' self-maintaining climax communities:

| | |
|---|---|
| Black spruce | Eastern hemlock |
| Red spruce | American beech |
| Northern white cedar | Sugar maple |
| Balsam fir | |

#### INTERMEDIATE

Wherever understory light is a little more abundant, the following species are able to compete successfully with the more tolerant species:

| | |
|---|---|
| White spruce | White ash |
| Red maple | Yellow birch |

#### INTOLERANT

Fast-growing pioneers, the following species are generally unable to survive in shade but persist in northern Appalachian forests as disturbance creates new openings for them:

| | | |
|---|---|---|
| Eastern white pine | Black cherry | Bigtooth aspen |
| Tamarack | Pin cherry | Balsam poplar |
| Paper birch | Quaking aspen | Gray birch |

ment of plants and animals. It has become a complex organization of producers and consumers. And in the late stages of succession the forest reaches a kind of dynamic equilibrium—like the pool in a stream that has a constant underlying flow of energy and materials into and out of it yet retains a stable organization and functional integrity within. In this equilibrium lies a certain resilience wherein small perturbations merely shift the flow of energy or nutrients from one pathway to another in the complex web, with little effect on the whole.

But although it is indeed a finely tuned ecosystem, the maturing forest can run down with age as nutrients are gradually depleted, sequestered for decades, even centuries, in the woody tissues of old trees, or leached out of the soil and carried downstream to other environments. In this aging condition the forest may eventually succumb to widespread outbreaks of insects or to wildfire; and such a fate may be considered of benefit in the long run, for disturbance of this nature releases locked-up nutrients and returns the forest to the young and vigorous. In the end, this recurring disturbance—not wanton destruction by human activity, but natural perturbations regulated by the shifting tides of energy within the system—preserves the great diversity of plant and animal species that make us all, knowing or not, so much the richer.

## *The Changing Fortunes of Animal Populations*

WITH THE DECLINE of agriculture in the Northeast after the middle of the nineteenth century and the dramatic reversal of land use throughout the region, many areas have reverted in less than one hundred years from as little as 20 percent to more than 80 percent forest cover. With this changing landscape some native animal species have experienced extreme fluctuations in number, from abundance to extirpation and back again. Some of the animals so prominent in the region's presettlement forests have vanished, perhaps forever, while others are doing better than ever before. And in at least one case, a new species has come on the scene to fill a niche vacated by the disappearance of another.

We have already noted that the large carnivores, the wolf and mountain lion (also referred to as the catamount or panther), were among the first to suffer from the pressures of expanding colonialism, and not without some concerted efforts on the part of early inhabitants to rid the countryside of them. That these animals were despised by our colonial ancestors is very clear in the latter's writings, which reveal a deep-seated fear of the animals and in many cases an unfortunate ignorance of the regulatory role they played in forest ecosystems. The mountain lion was considered, in the words of Zadock Thompson, to be the "most insidious and deadly foe of human kind," and wolves, it seems, were a close second. Of the latter, Thompson wrote in his *Natural History of Vermont* that "slaughter and destruction seemed their chief delight"; and he painted a picture of bands of wolves roving like street gangs, deliberately terrorizing neighborhoods and looking for trouble wherever they could find it.

Not surprisingly, the wolf and mountain lion carried heavy prices on their heads. The earliest record of a bounty in the New World goes back to 1630 in the Massachusetts colony, where the reward for killing a wolf was set according to the number of livestock in the settlement protected by the heroic deed. But large carnivores need large territories, and the rapid disappearance of habitat for both predator and prey brought about their demise more effectively than any bounty ever levied. In fact, the white-tailed deer, principal prey species of the wolf and mountain lion, was so decimated during the settling of the Northeast that as early as 1779 it had to be protected by law. Thus, by 1800, wolves too had become rare in central New York and New England and according to most accounts were completely extirpated from all but the remotest areas by the middle of the nineteenth century. Nonetheless, bounties were kept in effect into the twentieth century, and records show that the state of Vermont paid $20 on one wolf in 1894 and $36 on three wolves in 1902. In the Adirondack region, too, isolated wolf kills continued into the early 1900s.

The mountain lion also was considered to have been nearly extirpated by 1850, although apparently it held out a little longer in remote areas of the Adirondacks. Several were killed there in the late 1870s and the last recorded sighting was in 1894. The state of Vermont also paid a bounty of $20 on a mountain lion in 1895, and in Maine another was reported to have been shot as late as 1906.

Such, then, was the fortune of the big predators. Without adequate habitat, without a refugium within which a breeding population could be maintained, there could be little hope for these animals. But times are changing. Forest succession has come a long way since the turn of the twentieth century—not back to the forests of presettlement days, of course, but approaching a maturity and continuity that hasn't been seen for a long time. With the expanse of forest now stretching from northern New England through Quebec and the Maritime Provinces, it is interesting to speculate about whether these North Woods might again support the large carnivores.

The return of the mountain lion, in particular, seems an intriguing possibility. No doubt a certain mystique about this animal keeps it alive in the minds of woodsfolk; and reports of the big cat in the North Country have never ceased. Through the 1920s isolated accounts of mountain lions in New Hampshire were heard, and in

Vermont's Northeast Kingdom one was supposedly killed during that period. In 1926, two sightings of a mountain lion were reported in Huntington, Massachusetts, and a cast of a footprint taken in Chester, Vermont, in 1934 was later identified by the American Museum of Natural History as belonging to a mountain lion. Since 1950, reports of sightings in the northern Green Mountains have increased dramatically. The most recent accounts came in 1983, when a lion was allegedly sighted and its tracks measured at a deer carcass in Waitsfield, Vermont, and again in 1986, when an animal was reported in the vicinity of Waterville, Vermont.

The possibility of mountain lions slowly returning is perhaps not unrealistic given the expanse of uninterrupted forest in the northern Appalachians now and the abundance of prey species in the area, especially white-tailed deer. These cats are, after all, extremely wide-ranging and secretive animals, not often observed by humans even within their known range. A mountain lion on the move has been known to cover as much as 35 miles in a single night, so it should not seem incredible that one might at least occasionally wander through some remote corners of northern New England and the Adirondack region. Whether or not they are taking up residence, though, is still in debate. For all the reports, the mountain lion is not leaving much tangible evidence of its comings and goings—no trails in the snow, no scratchings in the litter, no scat. Until they do, their presence in the Northeast is only speculative. It is noteworthy, however, that while the state of New Hampshire still lists this species as "officially" extirpated, the Vermont Endangered Species Committee has recommended that the mountain lion be protected with endangered species status.

The possibility of the wolf's return to remote corners of our area might warrant speculation too, particularly with the road kill of an adult male gray wolf in the southern Adirondacks in 1968. However, it appears that a new predator, the eastern coyote, has already taken the wolf's place at the head of the food chain, and in nature, where law is established by the ebb and flow of energy between producers and consumers, there may not be room at the top for both.

The eastern coyote was first sighted in Vermont and New Hampshire in the early 1940s and has since spread widely throughout New England and upstate New York. This animal is not a "coydog," a hypothetical cross between a coyote or fox and some neglected, half-wild dog. It is an authentic species; a new predator that has arrived to fill a vacant niche in a landscape that for a while has been without a large predator. In essence the coyote is a sort of new wolf, a slightly smaller and more opportunistic animal better suited to the Northeast's forests of the twentieth century.

The best evidence against this animal's having a coyote-dog origin comes from crossbreeding siblings captured from the same litter of eastern coyotes. These crosses produce a second uniform litter, and the laws of genetics tell us that this is possible only if the original parents were of the same breed. A second-generation crossing of two distinctly different animals, like a coyote and domestic dog, would produce maximum variation of genetic character—some pups that looked like pure coyote and others that looked like the domestic mate. And some behavioral characteristics, too, argue against a coyote-dog cross; for example, observers have noted that the male of this species, unlike the domestic dog, cares for its young. It appears, indeed, that a new animal has evolved right before our eyes, possibly the result of crossbreeding between a northern subspecies of western coyote and the Ontario wolf, followed by a slow eastward migration and adaptation to a new environment.

Unfortunately, not everyone shares the excitement of finding a new species in our midst. The eastern coyote has already incurred the wrath of some, for it is, after all, partly carnivorous, and carnivores have never been popular, particularly in farm country. Coyotes have reportedly killed sheep, although I suspect with better reason than do the home-fed dogs that have also been known to kill sheep. And they surely will kill deer when they can. But dogs, people, and cars kill deer too, and the fact is that the eastern coyote is no match for a healthy white-tail. Time after time, autopsies of deer killed by coyotes reveal that previous injury, often a bullet wound, impaired the deer's mobility or reduced its stamina. Like all predators, the eastern coyote seeks easy prey, for it can't afford to expend too much energy chasing healthy quarry any distance; nor can it risk injury in a standoff against a much larger and stronger animal.

The eastern coyote simply lacks the makeup to be a marauding killer cast in the image of Thompson's misrepresented wolves, whose natural prey had been eliminated before they turned to livestock. This animal is much more of an opportunist, just as content raiding a garbage can or cleaning up the carcass of an animal that died of starvation as it is stalking mice or running down a sick deer. And its life style is apparently well suited to the Northeast's present countryside, for the coyote is enjoying considerable success, its numbers estimated in the thousands now throughout the northern Appalachians. The eastern coyote is a significant new contribution of the twentieth century, a product of landscape evolution as much as animal evolution, and it looks like it is here to stay, at least as long as our forests remain in their present condition.

If the Northeast's landscape is just right for this newcomer, it is also ready for a dramatic comeback of the wild turkey, a bird once so plentiful that it was the very symbol of bounty in the New World. Like so many of the other game animals native to the area, the turkey also had been exterminated in the Northeast by the middle of the 1800s. Certainly early New Englanders' insatiable appetite for this great bird contributed to its demise, but even without such hunting pressure it could not have survived the forest changes that have occurred over the last two hundred years.

The wild turkey is a bird of mature hardwood forests, not of corn fields or hedgerows or small disjunct woodlots. It had no place in the agricultural boom of the early 1800s, nor even in the postindustrial land-reversion era of the late 1800s, for neither its feeding preferences nor its survival skills lend themselves to early successional forests. The turkey makes its living primarily by scratching in the leaf litter for mast, and it depends on sharp eyesight in an open understory for evasion of predators. While it is also something of an opportunist—digging for tuberous roots, eating fruits and seeds from a number of plants, and even picking up insects and slugs when it finds them—the turkey depends heavily on the large seeds of the climax hardwood trees—acorns and hickory nuts in its southern range and beech nuts in the North Woods. When the mast crop is good, overwinter success is noticeably better and reproduction swings upward—when the crop is poor, the turkey suffers.

During difficult winters when the snow is deep and the mast crop has been poor, the turkey may derive some benefit by picking up seeds from the manure that northern hill farmers spread out over the snow. (One game biologist has referred to this as a hot-lunch program for turkeys.) But this bird's success today, following reintroduction only two decades ago, depends little on the helping hand of humankind. The story of the turkey's comeback is a story of forest succession, and if we have helped, it is through fifty years of cutting practice that has maintained the northern hardwoods as we now know them. The distribution of the wild turkey in the northern Appalachians today exceeds its precolonial range probably because the distribution of hardwood forest in the north exceeds its precolonial range; and this maturing forest is abundant with beech, thanks in part to selective cutting practices and a poor market for the wood of this tree.

As the wild turkey is prospering in our maturing hardwood forests, another familiar bird, the ruffed grouse, is not faring so well, for the ruffed grouse is something of an early successional counterpart to the turkey. Like the turkey, the overwinter success of the grouse depends heavily on a single preferred food source—in this case the buds of the pioneering quaking aspen. The grouse will feed on the buds of other tree species too, but aspen offers two distinct advantages: the buds, particularly of male flowers, provide an exceptionally high energy source, and the branches on which they are clustered are stout and easy to feed from. This enables the feeding grouse to fill its crop quickly while minimizing its exposure to predators, particularly owls (in the winter the grouse spends about fifteen minutes each evening, just before sundown, frantically filling its crop, and then dives into the snow where it spends the night digesting this energy). In our mature forests yellow birch is often the grouse's species of choice, but these trees have only small clusters of buds or catkins at the ends of flimsy branches, requiring much fluttering and commotion for food of comparatively low nutritive value. So the ruffed grouse is as dependent on early successional aspen groves as the turkey is on later successional forests. Regardless of whatever else is available, studies have shown that where there is no aspen in the forest canopy, grouse rarely overwinter successfully and breeding birds are seldom found. And aspen, being a short-lived pioneer species, is now dwindling in numbers as the forests that reclaimed the twentieth-century landscape pass into maturity and give way to the climax tree species. Forest succession, we see, plays a heavy hand in the fortunes of animal species too.

II.

# Plant Communities of the Adirondacks and Northern New England

At first glance, the complex mosaic of vegetation covering the hillsides and valleys of the northern Appalachian region may appear no more orderly than the random splotches of color on an artist's palette. But if we look closely, with an eye sensitive to subtle changes in shade and texture, we soon find that we can discriminate between different community types—the mottled greens of mixed hardwoods, the lighter shades of aspen groves, the soft, lacy texture of tamarack stands—and we begin to see patterns in the landscape that are not at all random. As we attempt to sort out these patterns, we find it possible to divide the landscape into a number of more or less discrete units, not unlike those of a jigsaw puzzle, but with an added dimension or two. The pieces of this puzzle are the plant communities themselves, associations of plant species that we recognize as belonging together under certain circumstances. In this puzzle, the pieces are put together according to topographic position; that is, the puzzle is assembled on a three-dimensional surface and each piece has its proper place depending on its particular site requirements. A lowland cedar community will not fit on a dry hillside, and a hillside beech-maple community will not interlock with fir on a high summit. But neither will the beech-maple community fit on a hillside dominated by an aspen-birch community, because the two represent different successional stages; that is, one normally precedes the other on a given site. So we have the added dimension of time in this puzzle.

Once we have the pieces of the puzzle sorted out—once we understand the basics of forest succession and how climate and local topography affect the distribution of vegetation types—then it becomes relatively easy to fit all the pieces together and to see in the landscape a great deal about its past history and present condition. Let's look, then, at the basic units of this puzzle and see how these communities are made up, how they function ecologically, and how they combine to form an integrated landscape.

## Spruce-Fir Woodlands

Spruce and fir dominate the forests of the cold hollows, of meandering stream flats, and of the higher mountain slopes throughout the northern Appalachians. The spruce-fir forest type, superbly adapted to the temperature and nutrient limitations of northern regions, is able to prosper under growing conditions that exclude most other tree species. Sites supporting these forests are generally nutrient poor, either because they receive very little nutrient input to begin with, as in the case of high-elevation forests, or because they are so cold that decomposer organisms responsible for the breakdown of organic matter are relatively ineffective. And the acidification of these soils by the conifer litter itself (conifer needles are very low in base ions) adds to the problem of

BALSAM FIR

*Needles are flat, of fairly uniform length and not sharply pointed. When stripped from a twig, the needles leave only a smooth, flat, and round abscission scar.*

scarcity, because some nutrients, like phosphorous, become insoluble and unavailable to plants under acid conditions.

The conifers have a considerable advantage on these sites. They conserve nutrients because they do not have to produce all new foliage every year (tamarack being the exception), and the evergreen habit of these species extends their photosynthetic season beyond that of deciduous trees, particularly in the spring of the year (as explained in the box on page 47). Furthermore, these trees can withstand winter temperatures of –80 degrees F and colder without injury, and many of the species prevalent in this forest type also can tolerate the flooded soils that often characterize lowland areas.

The different conifers that dominate our spruce-fir woodlands show fairly distinct site preferences and tend to segregate themselves along an elevational gradient from bottomland to treeline (as summarized in the box on page 41). Often the species that are most confusing to identify, like red spruce and black spruce, can be told apart just by the habitat they are found in. It is convenient, then, to talk about these trees and the communities they form in the order in which they occur along this

**BLACK SPRUCE**
*Needles are normally blue-green in color, relatively short, diamond-shaped in cross section and sharp-pointed. New twig ends are covered with very fine hairs. Cone scales have a ragged edge.*

gradient—as we might encounter them on a mountain trail.

Black spruce and balsam fir are the species of extremes and are found at both ends of this gradient. In the poorly drained flats of the northern lowlands, black spruce is usually abundant but may share dominance with balsam fir and others tolerant of wet soils, especially tamarack. Together these species make up the lowland conifer swamps, perhaps the most diverse of the spruce-fir community types. In these swamps the trees are rooted in a spongy organic soil that may be flooded part of the year, providing only a very shallow aerated zone for root activity. As a result, growth rates are slow and understory regeneration limited.

Black spruce often has the advantage in these moist environments, in that it reproduces quite readily by vegetative means. As lower branches come into contact with the mossy ground surface, roots develop from stem tissue no longer exposed to the air and sunlight, and the branches then turn upright to become self-sustaining

DISTRIBUTION OF CONIFERS IN THE NORTHERN APPALACHIANS.

*Specific in their site preferences, the northern conifers tend to segregate themselves along an elevational gradient. Black spruce is found at both ends of this gradient, wherever soils are organic, wet, and nutrient poor. In the lowland swamps balsam fir and tamarack usually accompany black spruce. White cedar, too, is most common in the wet bottomlands but generally lives along stream borders where it shows a preference for richer soils and better circulation of groundwater. White spruce, on the other hand, is a tree of higher ground in the northern sections of our region, requiring deeper soils with improved drainage. Hemlock also does better on higher ground where it usually occupies the less fertile but moister sites among the northern hardwood trees. Scattered about on the warmer soils of this zone, we find white pine too, a reminder of past disturbance in the hardwood forests. On the shallow, rocky soils of the middle and upper slopes, red spruce is the most abundant conifer, mixing with and gradually losing dominance to balsam fir at the higher elevations. While red spruce does reach the treeline, it is not nearly as well adapted to this extreme environment as is black spruce which, together with balsam fir, forms the prostrate "krummholz" (meaning "crooked wood") forest limit.*

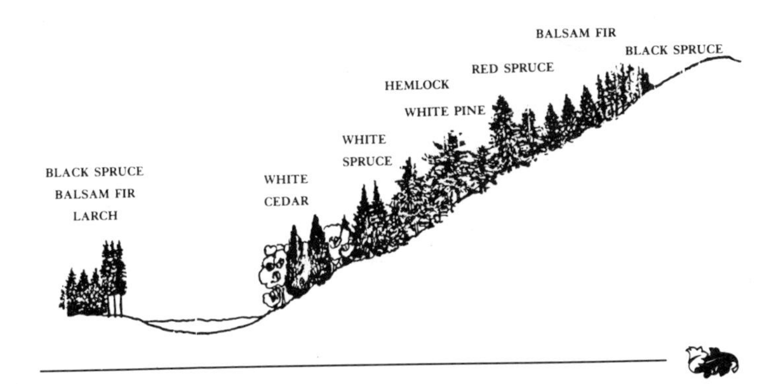

trees. Few other tree species can establish themselves under such swampy conditions, and even fir and larch may require a rotting log or stump to get started, because the ground often is too wet or acidic for successful seedling establishment.

With these constraints imposed by the cold, saturated soils, lowland spruce-fir forests tend to be less dense than the high-elevation forests. As a result, ample light reaches the forest floor, supporting the growth of many understory shrubs and herbaceous plants that give this forest community a richness of species lacking in other spruce-fir woodlands. Some of the more conspicuous shrubs of these lowlands are Labrador tea, low sweet blueberry and velvet-leaved blueberry, winterberry, black chokeberry, sheep laurel, and mountain holly. Among the herbaceous plants are a number of widespread northern species such as Canada mayflower, bunchberry, creeping snowberry, starflower, clintonia, goldthread, twinflower, and wood sorrel. In older stands where sufficient light reaches the inner branches of the canopy, the trees themselves often become draped with lichens (as described in the box on page 92), most notably the old man's beard that recalls the Spanish moss draping

CONIFERS FROM A DISTANCE

*Field guides generally rely on "hand-lens" characteristics for the identification of conifers—features like cone size, needle length and grouping, and presence or absence of hairs on twig ends. While these features are indispensable aids in many cases, other qualitative characteristics like profile, branching pattern, and foliage texture are useful in recognizing species from afar—from a mountaintop or even while you are wheeling down the interstate at 55 miles per hour. With practice, the common conifers of the North Woods can be identified easily from a distance. Here is what to look for.*

WHITE PINE

*Needles have a soft, almost fuzzy appearance from a distance, with foliage bunched toward the ends of twigs so that the overall texture might best be described as clumpy. The upper branches tend to arch strongly upward, spaced widely enough apart on older trees so that each branch can be distinguished from a distance.*

HEMLOCK

*Because the needles are attached singly and are uniformly distributed on the branches, hemlock overall has a very lacy texture. A spreading and somewhat disorganized branching pattern, often drooping near the ends, also gives it a shaggy look. Foliage thins out near the top of the tree, usually ending with a limp terminal leader that points in one direction or another (locals say it always bends toward the east—not unlikely because it has little resistance to winds that prevail from the west).*

BALSAM FIR

*This species' silhouette is its giveaway. When growing out in the open or reaching above the trees around it, the crown of balsam fir grows compactly and tapers sharply to a point, forming distinct, narrow "spires" against the sky. The foliage of balsam fir also tends to be predominantly blue-green.*

RED SPRUCE

*The branches and foliage of red spruce are stiff and erect, more like balsam fir in this respect than either white pine or hemlock, but with a more spreading form and rounded crown. Red spruce may be pyramidal in outline, but is looser and broader than balsam fir, not showing the spire form of the fir. The foliage of red spruce is normally dark olive-green.*

TAMARACK

*The foliage of tamarack is best described as wispy. Needles are short and clustered and give a very soft look to the crown, while branches are long and somewhat flimsy, adding to the wispy appearance. The color is usually pale green. In the fall, the needles turn pale gold, then drop, exposing a rather ragged profile during the winter that is mistakenly taken for dead by those unfamiliar with this tree's deciduous habit.*

*Now try your hand at identifying a few conifers from a distance. Identify the red spruce, balsam fir, and white pine in the photograph below. Then look ahead to Figure 8 and see if you can pick the tamarack out from the spruce and fir.*

the graceful oaks of the Deep South (Spanish "moss," though, is neither a moss nor a lichen but is actually a flowering vascular plant). In the Canadian boreal forest these lichens are an important source of food for foraging caribou in winter.

It should be noted in passing that white cedar, too, often occurs in wet areas, occasionally in pure stands (cedar swamps), but almost always along stream or pond margins where there is some circulation of groundwater. Cedar is less tolerant of the acidic conditions and low nutrient levels normally associated with the development of spruce-fir swamps.

On better-drained sites, black spruce is apparently unable to compete successfully with other species and is completely replaced by red or white spruce. In the northern border sections of Vermont, New Hampshire, and Maine, wherever soils are deep and well drained, white spruce often dominates. This species increases in abundance northward into the Canadian boreal forest but curiously does not extend its range into the subalpine forests of the northern Appalachians as do the many other boreal species that find a niche here. A few scattered

WHITE SPRUCE
*Needles are blue-green in color, relatively long, diamond-shaped in cross section, and sharp-pointed. New twig ends are completely hairless.*

individuals of white spruce have been found on the north side of Camel's Hump in Vermont, but there is reason to suspect that these were introduced.

Thus, on the middle slopes, red spruce is the most abundant conifer. It usually mixes with hemlock and hardwoods, but occasionally, where soils are poor, it is found in pure stands. Red spruce increases in number with elevation and generally becomes the dominant forest species in the lower reaches of the subalpine spruce-fir zone, at elevations around 3000 feet. Continuing upward, however, the relative abundance of red spruce and balsam fir shifts, with fir becoming dominant at elevations above 3500 feet. Thus we can distinguish a lower-elevation "spruce phase" and an upper-elevation "fir phase" in our subalpine forests. Red spruce may be found right up to treeline, but at the upper limit of tree growth in the northern mountains, black spruce reappears and together with balsam fir forms the krummholz zone of gnarled and matted trees.

It would be misleading to leave the impression here that spruce-fir woodlands consist of conifers only. In fact, hardwoods may comprise a minor part of the forest canopy almost anywhere. Paper birch, for example, is widely scattered throughout the range of spruce-fir hab-

## THE EVERGREEN ADVANTAGE

*It is commonly thought that the advantage of evergreen leaves to the plant lies in their being able to photosynthesize year-round. While this may be the case for evergreens in milder winter climates, available evidence indicates that it is not so for northern conifers. Photosynthesis in these trees appears to stop with the cessation of active growth and the onset of cold acclimation (the active process of acquiring tolerance to freezing) in the fall. Throughout most of the winter, the chloroplasts (the site of photosynthesis) in the conifer needle are found clumped together in an inactive state and remain devoid of any starch grains that would indicate photosynthetic activity. And no evidence suggests that the photosynthetic apparatus is able to reorganize itself and start up during brief periods of midwinter thaw. However, as early as mid-March starch begins to accumulate in the needles again, indicating that photosynthesis has resumed. Thus our conifers do have the advantage of being able to start up early and extend the usual photosynthetic season by six or eight weeks.*

*The primary advantage of the evergreen leaf, though, may be related to nutrient conservation. To understand how, let's think about plant growth in economic terms. Imagine a living plant as operating under the same constraints as any manufacturing business. In both cases, operating capital is invested in new machinery with the expectation of realizing a reasonable return on the investment. If working capital is in short supply, this machinery may have to be kept in service longer to maximize the investment return, even if the machinery becomes less efficient with age. The hard reality here is that only those with surplus capital can afford to reinvest regularly in new machinery.*

*In green plants, part of the investment capital used to construct photosynthetic machinery comes from the soil nutrient bank. This machinery then uses atmospheric carbon dioxide and light energy to provide high-energy carbohydrates that make possible additional growth in other parts of the plant. It takes nutrients, then, to build leaves, and if nutrients are in short supply, the evergreen leaf is a better investment for the simple reason that it lasts longer. The evergreen leaf is not quite as efficient photosynthetically, but it gives a return over a period of years and thus gives back more for the amount of nutrients invested. It is no coincidence that evergreens are commonly found growing in nutrient-deficient environments, for the evergreen habit conserves nutrients, and that may be its greatest advantage.*

---

itats right up to the treeline. The wetter sites at low elevations may also host scattered red maples, and along the river banks balsam poplar is often common (balsam poplar is the tree that flutters in the breeze and looks much like aspen, but has triangular leaves and a balsam fragrance). On the better-drained sites, quaking aspen often invades small openings. At higher elevations, mountain maple and mountain ash are common amid the conifers, as are shrubs like hobblebush, wild raisin, and mountain serviceberry.

An important aspect in the ecology of spruce-fir forests wherever they are found is repeated natural disturbance in one form or another. Windthrow is the most common

RED SPRUCE
*Needles are normally olive-green in color, sharp and diamond-shaped in cross section, and intermediate in length between black spruce and white spruce. New twig ends have numerous fine hairs. Cones are larger than those of black spruce and scales have smooth, not ragged, edges.*

disruptive force in the mature forest stand, owing to the shallow rooting of both red spruce and balsam fir. Breakage under heavy snow load is sometimes a common problem at high elevations, especially with balsam fir which does not produce as strong a wood as spruce and which also becomes susceptible to decay as it weakens in old age (old age is only seventy to eighty years in this species). As a result of this kind of disturbance, mature spruce-fir stands are often characterized by numerous small openings in the canopy.

The effects of disturbance on this vegetation can be varied, and depend not only on the nature and extent of the disturbance but also on the presence or absence of tree seedlings in the understory prior to disturbance. In some cases recurring disturbance contributes to the continual rejuvenation of the climax community. Because both red spruce and balsam fir are very shade tolerant and can maintain themselves for a long time under a closed canopy, the normal response to a sudden opening is the release of understory trees. It is not at all unusual to see these two species dominating such openings to the complete exclusion of all others. As long as there is adequate reproduction in the understory, disturbance on this scale (which might also include the selective cutting of trees) will maintain an equilibrium in the community, where mortality and reproduction are in continual balance. This process can slowly alter species composition, however, as sudden release almost always favors the more prolific and faster-growing balsam fir.

Where site conditions are well suited for the conifers and where reproduction by these species under the canopy is adequate, the spruce-fir community may be quite stable and resistant to change. In the absence of understory regeneration, however, any disturbance to this community may bring about a major shift in vegetation type. On better-drained sites an opening of the canopy, especially if accompanied by scarification of the soil, may result in the rapid influx of intolerant and fast-growing hardwoods, principally paper birch, yellow birch, pin cherry, and mountain maple. Lacking competition from conifer reproduction, these hardwoods grow vigorously and may occupy the site for a considerable length of time; the period depends primarily on the condition of the sub-

A.

FIGURE 7 *What happens to a spruce-fir woodland after disturbance depends largely on the condition of the understory and on the nature of the disturbance itself. Where understory regeneration by spruce and fir is abundant (a) and disturbance is of a local nature, such as by windfall, then the stand may be quite resilient. This particular stand is at an elevation of about 3500 feet and is essentially self-maintaining (note the decaying birch log in the foreground, a remmant of an earlier stage in succession). However, should this stand be subjected to large-scale disturbance, such as by fire, it would likely be invaded by paper birch, the principal pioneer species at that elevation. Paper birch would dominate for several decades, but would eventually yield to spruce and fir again (b). At lower elevations, disturbance by logging leads to invasion of the site by aggressive hardwoods like pin cherry and yellow birch (c), but here, too, we see spruce and fir saplings appearing amid the dense regeneration, and if left alone they will eventually regain dominance of the site.*

strate. If the soil is deep and well drained, the later seeding in of shade-tolerant sugar maple and beech could eventually bring about a long-term change in cover type, a change that we have witnessed in so many logged-over areas throughout northern New England and the Adirondacks. If the site is of poorer quality, the stand of successional hardwoods may be only temporary, with the conifers eventually reassuming dominance (*Figure 7*).

B.

C.

## Heath Bogs

Here and there, the spruce-fir forests open up into treeless glades—an old beaver meadow, perhaps, where grasses and sedges have colonized the mud flats behind a broken dam, or a bog where heath shrubs and sphagnum moss have woven a dense mat of vegetation over still water. A certain sense of excitement comes with unexpectedly encountering these backwaters of the boreal forest—an excitement spurred by the anticipation of finding a rare orchid or surprising a cow moose and her calf browsing on pond weeds. It's a just anticipation, because these open areas are uncommon habitats and uncommon habitats often hold rare sights.

The orchid and the moose are not always found in the same place, however, for their natural preferences differ, and there are several important distinctions between the marsh flooded by beaver activity, where we are likely to see the moose, and a heath bog, where we are apt to find the orchid. In fact, in many respects the two habitats are quite opposite. The marsh is richer in nutrients and therefore supports much more productive plant growth, and it often teems with wildlife—mammals, birds, amphibians, and fish. The bog, on the other hand, is nutrient poor and highly acidic, so that only a relatively few plant species live there, and its animal life is mostly transient, finding little reason to take up residence. That both of these wetland types may develop within the same stretch of boreal forest, though, compels us to ask what makes for such differences in physical and biological nature between the two habitats. Why is it that some wet spots become marshes or swamps and others bogs?

The character of a wetland is determined in large part by the degree of water moving through it. Groundwater circulation improves nutrient relations either because it increases the importation of minerals from outside the area or because it increases the contact between water and soil particles, aiding in nutrient exchange. Improved nutrient relations generally mean more species, greater productivity (that is, more solar energy captured by plants), and more energy moving through the food web. The most fundamental difference between a marsh and a bog, then, has to do with groundwater movement. Bogs develop where groundwater circulation is blocked, where flow-through is negligible, and where nutrient input is primarily—sometimes entirely—via rainwater. Through marshes, on the other hand, there is always some circulation of water, however imperceptible it may be. Even if water has been impounded by beavers, flow-through is sufficient to maintain a higher nutrient status than in a bog.

These conditions translate into distinct differences between the two wetlands in soil type and plant cover. The soils of bogs consist entirely of undecomposed organic matter, reflecting a general lack of microbial activity, and it is often possible to identify plant remains several hundred years old. In contrast, the rate of decomposition in marshes is more rapid and, although marsh soil is richly organic, it contains little of recognizable plant remains. The term *muck*, as used by soil scientists, describes marsh soil perfectly.

The vegetation supported by these two wetland types is strikingly different too, and one can tell at a glance what is going on beneath the surface just by the presence or absence of a few key species. Cattails in standing water always indicate nutrient enrichment, whereas a preponderance of evergreen shrubs and sphagnum moss around the water's edge indicates a low-nutrient environment (see *Figures 8 and 9*).

Many of the bogs that we encounter in the northern Appalachians are floating-mat or "quaking" bogs, having

## *Wetlands at a Glance*

### BOG

*Groundwater:*
- no circulation
- water level remains at or below vegetated surface for most of the growing season

*Soil:*
- partly or wholly undecomposed organic matter with plant remains often identifiable; in floating-mat bogs, sediment accumulates from the surface down
- nutrient poor
- highly acidic

*Vegetation:*
- dominated by sphagnum, sedges, and heath shrubs

*Animal life:*
- few species, mostly insect; birds and mammals largely transient

### MARSH

*Groundwater:*
- circulation important
- water level remains at or above vegetated surface for much of the growing season

*Soil:*
- well-decomposed organic matter mixing with mineral soil; sediment accumulating from the bottom up
- improved nutrient availability
- less acidic than bogs

*Vegetation:*
- dominated by grasses and floating-leaved aquatic plants

*Animal life:*
- great diversity of animal species including aquatic birds, mammals, reptiles, and amphibians

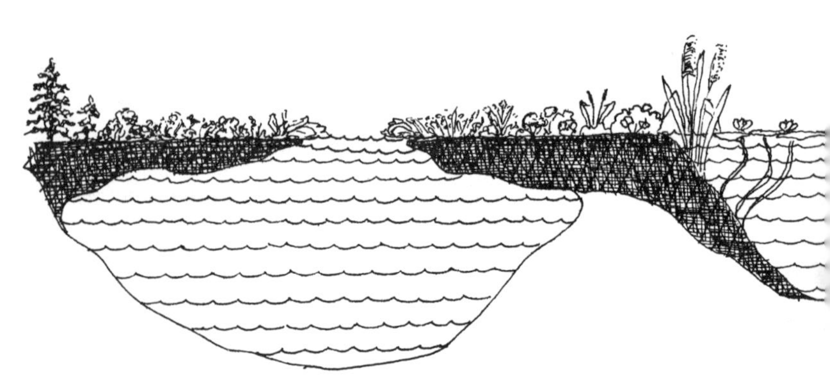

## SWAMP

*Groundwater:*
- circulation important
- ground saturated if not flooded, usually with standing water in depressions

*Soil:*
- partly to well-decomposed organic matter mixing with some mineral sediment
- improved nutrient availability
- usually more acidic than marshes, less acidic than bogs

*Vegetation:*
- dominated by trees and tall shrubs (note that a bog in late stages of succession may also be sparsely treed)

*Animal life:*
- diverse animal populations

FIGURE 8 *Differences in vegetative character between bogs and marshes are determined largely by nutrient availability, which in turn is affected by groundwater circulation. The open channel through this marsh clearly indicates groundwater movement, however sluggish, but even ignoring the channel, the plants tell of improved nutrient relations. The alders and aquatic grasses lining this open water are typical of wetlands receiving added nutrients either through a more rapid breakdown of organic and mineral matter owing to water-soil exchange or through seepage from surrounding areas. Compare this example with the bog vegetation shown in* Figure 9.

their origin in kettle holes left by the disappearance of buried glacial ice some 12,000 years ago. The development of a quaking bog over open water in these kettles does not depend on sedimentation and basin filling, as is often the case with a marsh, but rather involves the progressive development—over a period of centuries—of a mat of vegetation that floats over the water and accumulates organic matter, building in thickness downward from the water's surface. The primary mat-forming species in our area is leatherleaf, a woody shrub that commonly invades still water and pond shores (*Figure 9a*). As this plant branches out over the open water, the increasing weight of foliage depresses the older branches below the water's surface, stimulating new shoot growth and forming a dense tangle of branches. In a similar fashion, sweet gale and buckbean may also weave a mat over the water. The accumulation of litter on this framework of branches eventually creates a floating substrate suitable for colonization by other plants, most often led by sphagnum moss and a few species of aquatic sedges that are tolerant of acidic conditions. Pitcher plants and sundew may then follow, and as consolidation of the mat progresses with the accumulation of sphagnum peat, other heath shrubs become established (*Figure 9b*). By this time in the bog's succession, the mat will usually hold the weight of an adult, but it will quiver as you walk across it, like a giant waterbed, and will remain a "quaking" bog until it finally fills to the bottom with organic matter and solidifies.

The invasion of a wet site by leatherleaf does not, by itself, set the direction of succession. If physical influences like fluctuating water levels or a change in nutrient status favor the growth of floating pond weeds or emergent aquatic vegetation, the site might still develop into a marsh. However, once sphagnum mosses become established, the direction of succession becomes irrevocably set, provided that no significant outside influences intervene. This is because sphagnum moss (*Figure 10a*), more than any other species, reinforces all those conditions that make a bog what it is. For one thing, sphagnum has an extraordinary capacity to retain water. So absorbent is it that it has long been used by northern peoples as a natural diaper material—collected, dried, and packed around the infant in a cradle board. Sphagnum can hold ten times its own weight in water. In addition, sphagnum moss has a rapid growth rate and accumulates very quickly in the bog because of the lack of decomposition. This combination of rapid accumulation and high ab-

A.

FIGURE 9 *Leatherleaf growing in still water (a) is a precursor to the development of a heath bog. The pioneering evergreen shrub, which is tolerant of low-nutrient conditions, forms a dense tangle of branches over open water; the tangle holds litter and eventually provides a floating mat upon which other plants adapted to this kind of environment may take root. In photograph (b), behind the leading edge of leatherleaf sphagnum moss is invading, along with a few sedges and other heath shrubs that give the bog its unique character.*

B.

A.

FIGURE 10 *Sphagnum moss (a), more than any other species, makes the bog what it is. By its rapid growth rate and high water-absorbing capacity, this plant contributes to the retention of water and restriction of its circulation. Sphagnum also is responsible for acidification of the water, which renders some nutrients insoluble and further reinforces the nutrient impoverishment that characterizes a bog. Some plants, like the round-leaved sundew (b), deal with this restriction by capturing insects to supplement their nutrient intake.*

B.

sorptive capacity means that sphagnum helps retain water and greatly reduces its movement through the bog.

But perhaps the most important influence of sphagnum moss in directing succession lies in its ability to acidify the environment in which it grows. Sphagnum has an extraordinary capacity to exchange positively charged atoms (cations) in the bog water, absorbing nutrients like calcium and replacing them with hydrogen ions, leaving the water acidified in the process (acidity, remember, is a measure of hydrogen ion concentration). The resulting acidity inhibits microbial activity and creates nutrient-stress problems for plants not adapted to such conditions (*Figure 10b*). I have seen situations where the open water at the center of a bog was actually alkaline, with a pH of 8.0, while less than 30 feet away, where sphagnum was invading the floating mat, the pH was down to 3.8—acid enough to preserve anything that might fall into it! Thus sphagnum in effect inhibits its own decomposition.

Eventually, scattered individuals of black spruce and tamarack may become established on the mature bog mat, but the question is still open whether or not succession will proceed in the end to a spruce-fir forest com-

DOUBLE-DEALING PLANTS

*No other plant that I can think of epitomizes adaptation in the natural world quite like the pitcher plant. Within the vat of its highly evolved leaves, this plant harbors its own living microcosm, a miniature ecosystem, superimposed on the stingy substrate of the sphagnum bog.*

*The pitcher plant obtains its energy through photosynthesis, but like all green plants, it must extract nutrients from the soil or rainwater to build protein and other essential plant compounds. The bog, we know, is not very generous in this regard,*

*but the pitcher plant has found two ways to overcome the problem of nutrient shortage.*

*The adaptation that we are most familiar with is its insectivorous habit. Beneath its liver-colored flowers (said to attract carrion-feeding insects) the plant lays an eloquent trap. In the course of evolution its leaves have curled and fused to form a receptacle that arches gracefully upward to catch rainwater; but it is not water alone that the plant consumes. These unique leaves are equipped with their own nectaries to attract insects and with other devices to ensure that once attracted, the visitors will not leave again. Hundreds of downward-pointing hairs around the lip of the leaf make it easy for an insect to descend into the pitcher but nearly impossible for it to crawl back out against the grain. Below the throat of the pitcher, epidermal cells exude a sticky substance and slough off easily, attaching to the insect's feet and further inhibiting its escape. The struggling insect slips into the water at the bottom of the pitcher and soon drowns, to be digested through the actions of enzymes the plant secretes into the water.*

*The insectivorous habit of this and other plants of similar environments, including sundew, provides an important supplement to the scant supply of nitrogen in a bog. But the pitcher plant does not leave nutrient procurement only to the chance capture of insects. Within the body of water held in the leaf, thriving populations of bacteria grow, their entire world that little vat of enriched rainwater. And recent studies have shown that nitrogen-fixing bacteria, those with the special ability to convert atmospheric nitrogen to a form suitable for plant uptake, are regular constituents of the pitcher's aquatic community and that the levels of nitrogen found in leaf tissues of the pitcher plant could be accounted for by bacterial activity alone.*

*So the pitcher's little world is a much more complicated system than meets the eye, and close observation reveals still more going on within this microcosm, where many other organisms take advantage of the pitcher plant's unique adaptations. It has been found, for example, that one species of mosquito actually breeds in the water within the leaf, its larvae maturing there before taking leave as winged adults; that a small moth also lays its eggs exclusively on the pitcher plant so that its larvae can mature within the protection of the newly developing leaf cavities while actually feeding on the interior epidermal cells; and that some species of spiders spin webs across the opening of the pitcher to intercept insects destined to nourish one or the other, plant or spider. So should you encounter a pitcher plant, take a few minutes to examine a leaf closely, without disturbing it. You may witness a lot of drama within this miniature ecosystem.*

munity, as classical textbooks often suggest. Once the mat is formed, it is likely to remain unchanged for a relatively long time, because as peat accumulates, the mat is depressed by its increased weight, and habitat conditions at the surface change little. In effect, the physical instability of the floating mat contributes significantly to the biological stability of the bog community. The number of plants that can tolerate the conditions of the bog habitat is so limited that species replacement, as we have described it in talking about floristic relay succession, does not occur on the mat itself, and only the filling of the basin under the mat may make possible the invasion of the site by conifers tolerant of the low pH (*Figure 11*). Conditions on the mat may stave off this colonization by tree species for a long time, though, because the bog, largely by virtue of the characteristics of the sphagnum moss, is so self-perpetuating. Recently, in fact, it has been discovered that one of the common bog shrubs, sheep laurel, releases a chemical that specifically inhibits root development in black spruce. The exact source and identity of the compound is still unknown, but it seems

FIGURE 11 *Bog succession is often described as ending with the invasion of the site by conifers like black spruce and tamarack. The characteristics of sphagnum moss alone, however, make the bog self-perpetuating, and it may resist such invasion for a long time. In this photograph a small tamarack has become established on the bog mat, but its foothold is tenuous and may be ahead of its time. Most likely, succession to a spruce or tamarack swamp here will proceed slowly inward from the edges of the bog as the organic substrate solidifies.*

that this one plant, and perhaps others yet to be discovered, protects its own interests and contributes further to the bog's longevity.

Not all bogs originate in kettle holes. Many in our area form in shallow bedrock depressions at high elevations where rainfall provides adequate moisture to support bog vegetation. Perhaps the most numerous and extensive of these bogs are found along the ridge tops of the Mahoosuc Range, on the Maine-New Hampshire border (*Figure 12a*), where they are couched among drier "heath balds" (the origin of the latter, which are plant communities dominated by sheep laurel and other heath shrubs, is not completely understood). These ridge-top bogs are often colonized first by a moss called *Drepanocladus fluitans* (it has no common name) and by a tussock-forming alpine plant called deer's hair sedge, which seems to prefer wet or disturbed soils (*Figure 12b*). This early successional stage may bear little resemblance to the pioneering plant community of low-elevation bogs, but these two species pave the way for others like the round-leaved sundew and small bog cranberry, and eventually sphagnum moss invades and the bog begins to take on a familiar look. Once sphagnum has become established, the direction of succession is similar to that at low elevations, except for the addition of a few new species like alpine bilberry, black crowberry, and a dwarf raspberry called cloudberry.

The principal sphagnum species in our subalpine bogs is *Sphagnum fuscum* (again, no common name), which is leather-brown in color and has very small, tightly clustered leaves that give it a manicured and cushiony appearance. This species, too, has a very rapid growth rate, considering the environment it grows in, and nearly engulfs the other plants that grow in the bog with it. In fact, where the bog is dominated by *Sphagnum fuscum* the heath shrubs appear much smaller than usual and pro-

A.

FIGURE 12 *High-elevation bogs may be encountered most anywhere in mountains of the northern Appalachian region, but are nowhere more extensive than on the ridge tops of the Mahoosuc Range in Maine (a). Ridge-top bogs owe their origin to the accumulation of water in shallow bedrock depressions and initial colonization of these sites by the moss* Drepanocladus fluitans *and a tussock-forming alpine plant, the deer's hair sedge (b). These two species pave the way for invasion of the site by* Sphagnum fuscum, *which thereafter controls the direction of succession through its effects on soil accumulation, acidification, and water retention.*

B.

THE WOOLLY LEAF PARADOX *That many northern bog plants should share so much in common with arid land plants seems a striking contradiction; yet the thick waxy leaves of leatherleaf and sheep laurel, the narrow rolled-under leaves of bog rosemary and bog laurel, and the dense woolly underside of Labrador tea all represent classic water-conserving adaptations. Each of these features is designed to increase the resistance of the leaf to the outward diffusion of water vapor, thereby reducing water loss when the supply is limited. The obvious question, then, is why, when they are growing with their roots in water, do these plants display such adaptations?*

LABRADOR TEA

*For many decades this question led ecologists to hypothesize a condition of physiological drought in bogs, suggesting that even though water appears plentiful, it is not available to the plants. The reason, they speculated, is somehow related to the high acidity and low oxygen content of the bog water, which perhaps inhibited root uptake. However, studies made possible by more recent technological advances have disproved most of these theories, and it now appears that water conservation may be important to these plants only secondarily.*

*The one other characteristic that these bog plants have in common with each other is that they are evergreen, and evergreen leaves, as described in the box on page 00, are of advantage in nutrient-deficient environments where their longevity results in a greater yield of photosynthate per unit of nutrient invested in their construction. And few environments are as nutrient deficient as the bog, for input is limited almost entirely to rainwater—not a particularly rich source—and the high acidity of the bog further reduces the availability of some elements. But life is full of trade-offs, and the big risk that the evergreen plant faces is excessive water loss from sun-exposed foliage during winter, when the supply of water from cold or frozen soils is restricted. This is where the water-conserving adaptations play a role. In bog plants, then, the evergreen habit is apparently the primary adaptation—a nutrient-conservation strategy—and the water-conserving adaptations are a secondary development, helping to get the evergreen leaf safely through the winter.*

vide only sparse ground cover; poking beneath the surface, though, reveals that these are not dwarfed shrubs at all, but rather only the very tips of branches reaching for daylight. Whole plants, buried by the sphagnum, are just managing to keep a few leaves above the surface. The moss layer rises about 1 centimeter each year, and the growth rate of the other plants barely matches that!

In the subalpine bogs of the higher ridge tops, *Sphagnum fuscum* is responsible for yet another interesting feature—the preservation of frozen peat lenses beneath the surface. These windswept ridges are blown clear of snow throughout much of the winter, and without that protective cover, soils freeze right to bedrock. When the thick sphagnum cushion dries at the surface during the following summer, it becomes a very good insulator and keeps the peat beneath from thawing completely. The frozen lenses may persist throughout the summer and into fall, maybe lasting year-round in some cases, and no doubt have a very important influence on succession in these bogs. Apart from inhibiting nutrient-cycling processes, such cold soils would surely impair root development in any invading conifer seedlings. So again we find that these bog habitats are very stable, largely through the self-perpetuating role of sphagnum.

## Northern Hardwood Forests

How much poorer we would be without our deciduous broadleaf forests—without their spring show of ephemeral wildflowers and their cool green summer shade; without the exuberance of their fall colors, the smell of dried leaves, and that sense of season that keeps us in touch with the rhythms of the natural world. And when the leaves are down and the skies gray with the first snows of November, these same hardwoods—the sugar maple, beech, and yellow birch—keep us warm around the wood stove, for no conifer gives back as much heat in winter.

The deciduous forests add much to the diversity of our landscape. These are the forests of intermediate site conditions, of deeper, better-drained soils; forests of the middle ground between the extremes of the cold, wet bottomlands and the rocky, windswept subalpine slopes; forests that harbor a wealth of plant and animal species that find the coniferous woods lacking for one reason or another.

The sugar maple and beech that dominate these woodlands are not unique to the Northeast; their ranges actually go far south, extending all the way down the Appalachians and the Mississippi Valley into Georgia and Arkansas. But in the northern Appalachians these two species, together with yellow birch, form a distinctive community that we call the northern hardwood association. Of course these species are not alone in this community. Other maples—striped or goosefoot, mountain, and red—along with black and pin cherry, white ash, and paper birch are also common in the mature northern hardwood forest. And it is not a community of hardwoods only, as the name might suggest. White pine is scattered widely about, a persistent remnant of earlier

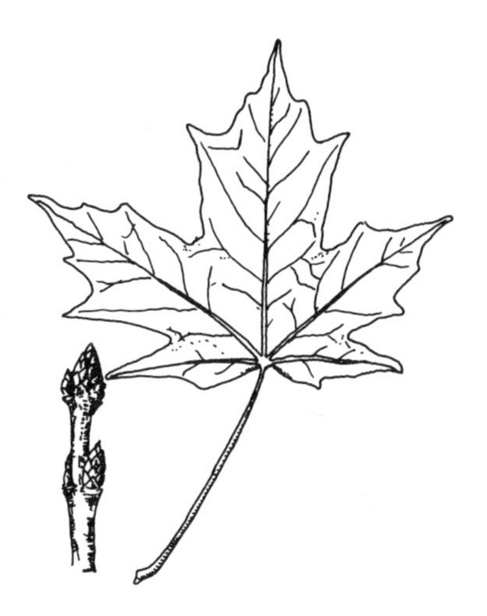

SUGAR MAPLE
*Note that interlobes are U-shaped and the leaf margin is not saw-toothed. Buds on leafless twigs are small, narrow, and pointed, and brown in color.*

successional stages often seen silhouetted against the skyline, as on many lower ridge tops in the Adirondacks. Hemlock and red spruce are important constituents of these woods too, perhaps even more so in earlier days than in our present second- or third-growth forests; and in many places today balsam fir can be seen establishing itself in the understory. By and large, though, the sugar maple, beech, and yellow birch dominate the northern

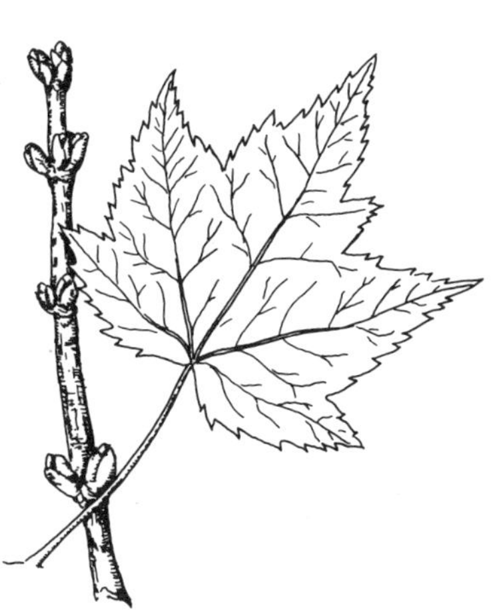

RED MAPLE
*Interlobes are V-shaped and the leaf margin is sharply toothed. Buds are larger than the sugar maples, rounded, and clustered at the twig end, and somewhat reddish in color.*

hardwood forests and give them the special character that is known nowhere else in the United States.

It is to a large extent the seasonality of these three deciduous trees that sets the tempo of life in the northern hardwood forests. For many of the small perennials of the forest floor, the growing season is compressed between the time when snow cover disappears and the days when the hardwood canopy closes over with new summer leaves. The forest canopy acts as a filter affecting not just the quantity of light reaching the forest floor, but also its quality—its suitability for photosynthesis; so for many of the ephemeral herbs, springtime is a race to complete their life cycle before light becomes too limiting. Some species even begin their growth under the snowpack, channeling last year's starch reserves into new tissue and manufacturing chlorophyll under the weak blue light that filters down through the snow. The familiar trout lily and spring beauty are among the first of the ephemeral herbs to appear, sometimes flowering within a couple of days after being released from the snowpack. But barely six weeks later the plants can scarcely be found, for they have done what they were programmed to do and have put away sufficient carbohydrate in their underground corms to carry them through to another spring.

The hardwood trees themselves are also geared to maximum energy conversion during a relatively short growing season. If the evergreen conifer is likened to the long-term enterprise, using resources conservatively for a return over a longer period, then the deciduous broadleaf tree is the opportunist looking for a quick return on its investment. The deciduous hardwood must produce its entire photosynthetic machinery anew each year and must get sufficient return from it not only to pay back the energy costs of construction and maintenance but also to support new growth of the tree. And because the

FALL COLORS

*The green leaves of summer harbor more than meets the eye, for beneath their veil of chlorophyll hides an impressive array of colorful pigments—carotenoids and phycobilins that are yellow, orange, and red. We don't see much of these pigments in summer because they are swamped by the sheer abundance of chlorophyll, but they are present throughout the season and serve an important function in the leaf. These "accessory" pigments trap light in portions of the spectrum not absorbed by chlorophyll and transfer this energy to the chlorophyll molecules, thereby increasing the efficiency of the photosynthetic process.*

*In the fall of the year, when temperatures drop, chlorophyll molecules in deciduous leaves begin to break down and are no longer replaced. Only then are the brilliant colors of the other pigments unmasked. And as growth processes throughout the tree slow and the translocation of metabolites out of the leaves diminishes, sugars that are no longer in demand accumulate in the leaves, where they stimulate production in some species of yet another nonphotosynthetic pigment called anthocyanin. Anthocyanin is bright red in color and is produced in the vacuole or central void of the epidermal cells that make up the leaf's outer layers. Oddly, anthocyanin apparently benefits the leaf little at this time of year (it has no known function in the senescing leaf), but it certainly does much for us as it fires the fall colors that dress our hardwood forests in magnificence.*

hardwood tree sheds its leaves each fall, it has to bank enough carbohydrate during the summer to support the flush of new leaves the following year. Unlike the conifer, the hardwood has no older foliage from which it can borrow photosynthetic reserves to fuel the spring start up. The tree is equal to its task, however. Compared to the evergreen leaf, the hardwood leaf generally has a thinner wax coating (a benefit of not having to protect the leaf all winter) and many more stomates, the tiny pores through which carbon dioxide and water vapor pass. It is therefore nearly ten times more efficient than the conifer needle in obtaining atmospheric carbon dioxide for photosynthesis. What the hardwood leaf lacks in longevity, then, it seems to make up for in increased photosynthetic efficiency, and its ability to produce surplus energy reserves is evidenced by the presence of large stores of sugars in the tree that are mobilized and translocated to budding shoots as the days of spring warm above freezing—stores that we can tap for syrup production with little effect on the tree. It is noteworthy that the healthy hardwood tree generally produces enough surplus that it can withstand one or two complete defoliations from insect infestation before it runs out of reserves for the production of additional foliage. And all of this reserve energy is accumulated during a growing season of at best three months.

We noted in the opening chapter that the present expansiveness of northern hardwood forests in upstate New York and northern New England is due in large part to the history of logging activity in this region. Although something of an artifact in many locations, these forests nonetheless are very stable communities on the better-drained sites throughout the northern Appalachians and are, no doubt, there to stay for a while. Many opportunistic species in this community quickly fill and stabilize small openings in the forest, and the community dominants are shade tolerant and able to maintain themselves for a long time. The notion of stability, though, should not conjure up images of static forests, never changing in composition under the closed canopy. The three forest dominants themselves differ markedly in their reproductive strategies, so that over time their position relative to each other changes. Yellow birch is the most mobile of the group (as is paper birch at the higher

YELLOW BIRCH
*The leaf margin is double-toothed (small teeth superimposed on a pattern of larger teeth). Freshly broken twigs have a wintergreen aroma.*

elevations), producing large quantities of very light seeds that get around the forest quite well. And when the opportunity arises—when an old giant of a sugar maple finally crashes to the ground—the yellow birch is there and grows quickly in the new opening. Skid roads from logging operations often provide an ideal seed bed for birch, as in the view from Mount Lafayette described in the preface, and on the distant hillsides one can often see thin lines of a different green extending into the spruce woods—yellow birch and paper birch recording the history of logging activity for the discerning eye to read. Within the hardwood forests, then, the distribution of yellow birch is often patchy and the patches shift about over time because yellow birch does not reproduce as well in its own shade as the other occupants.

Beech is much less opportunistic than yellow birch in its reproductive strategy. Instead of releasing large quantities of mobile seeds, it produces far fewer and much larger seeds. The familiar beech nut doesn't get around very well, but it stores large energy reserves to improve its chances of success where it does germinate, which is often in the shade of the parent tree. With all their stored food, beech nuts are also attractive to many foraging an-

AMERICAN BEECH

*Note the coarsely saw-toothed leaf margins, with parallel veins ending at the tip of each tooth. Buds on leafless twigs are very long and lance shaped.*

imals—squirrels, wild turkeys, bears—which of course offsets some of their other advantages. However, as if to add a little insurance, the beech also has a habit of cloning—producing sprouts from roots—in many circumstances, which is an ideal way of holding on to a favorite site. So between their heavy seeds and occasional root sprouting, beech trees, once established, tend to be more stable over time in spatial distribution.

This is not to suggest that beech will occupy a given site forever, though. Like all trees, beech may succumb to any number of problems with aging (see the box on page 75) and many other species may be marking time nearby, ready to grow into a new opening. The shade-tolerant hemlock and red spruce, for example, may persist for years in the understory, waiting their turn. And invisible but omnipresent seed of pioneer species often lies buried and viable until some disturbance removes the organic litter and triggers its germination. Pin cherry, an early colonizer that lives only about thirty years, may produce five million seeds per acre from a dense stand, which are then distributed widely by foraging birds. These seeds remain viable in the soil for more than fifteen years and germinate quickly with disturbance, springing up as if through spontaneous generation when no other

## BEECH BARK DISEASE

*Many older stands of beech in the Northeast have suffered serious dieback in recent years, the result of a wave of beech bark disease that moved through the area in the 1950s and 1960s. Beech bark disease is a pathological condition actually involving two different attack organisms, neither of which by itself would likely cause the death of a tree. The disease starts when tiny, wingless insects called woolly beech scale invade a tree, quite often an aging or injured tree, and begin feeding on the bark. These insects resemble aphids in their manner of feeding, inserting a sucking stylet into living bark tissues, and like the aphid, they produce a woolly white wax covering that is usually the first visible evidence of their presence. In large numbers, these insects bring about the death of bark tissues as they tap the living cells for metabolites. This condition leads to cracking of the bark and eventual invasion by another organism known as the canker fungus. This fungus parasitizes the bark tissue too, and may eventually girdle the tree. The conspicuous pink coloring of the bark by numerous tiny red fruiting bodies of the canker fungus is sure evidence that the bark of the tree has been killed. By this point decay fungi may have already entered the wood, perhaps with secondary wood-boring insects, and the weakened bole is susceptible to breakage in the wind, a phenomenon known as beech snap.*

*Beech scale was accidentally introduced into Nova Scotia from Europe in the late 1800s and has slowly pushed its way south and west. The first wave of beech bark disease had progressed through northern New England and into the Adirondacks by 1960 and has now reached southern Pennsylvania and western New York State. In the aftermath of the resulting dieback, the abundance of beech in many places has actually increased with saplings that sprouted from the roots of affected trees. Young trees are usually more resistant than older ones, but many of these second-generation thickets, the vegetative progeny of diseased trees, have already become infested with another scale insect,* Xylococculus betulae, *that creates wounds on which the woolly beech scale (now a permanent resident in the Northeast), and later the canker fungus, can get established. Because the woolly beech scale is present throughout the Northeast now and is dispersed primarily by the wind, new local outbreaks of beech bark disease can erupt almost anywhere in the area. Here and there, however, apparently resistant trees have survived the initial wave, which along with the persistent root sprouting of diseased trees, gives hope that the beech will not go the way of the disease-ravaged American chestnut and American elm.*

pin cherries are left around. In hardwood stands over one hundred years old, where pin cherry has long since disappeared, as many as forty thousand seeds of this species per acre may lie buried in the soil, waiting their time. Red maple, paper birch, and yellow birch, each with seed longevity of up to fifteen years too, are also well represented in the buried seed pool of the forest floor, and they crop up very quickly after disturbance. Paper birch, in particular, appears to proliferate after fire, especially at upper elevations, and occasionally one will come across large and nearly pure stands of this species whose origin was associated with a burn. A look around in the litter layer of these stands will often reveal old fire-scarred stumps or charcoal in the soil.

When we talk about stability in a climax northern hardwood forest, then, we don't mean to imply a static condition. To be sure, the dominant sugar maple, beech, and yellow birch are long-lived and could potentially occupy a site for a time measured in centuries. But if we could observe a landscape long enough, we would see a slowly continuing internal reorganization, with beech growing up under sugar maple, sugar maple seeding in under yellow birch, and yellow birch reestablishing itself in new openings. The climax northern hardwood forest,

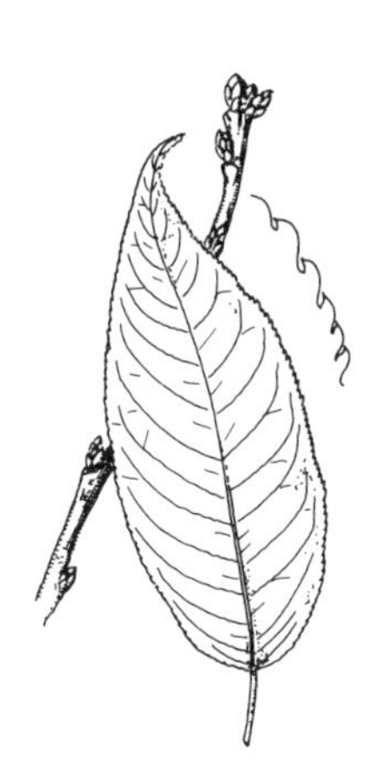

**PIN CHERRY**
*All species of cherry have a characteristic pungent odor when leaves or twigs are crushed. Note the tiny recurved teeth on the leaf margin of the pin cherry.*

then, represents a dynamic equilibrium, always changing, but on a larger scale always the same.

When you walk through the northern hardwoods now, take note of what is going on in the understory. Is the forest multistoried, consisting of trees of all sizes, as if undisturbed for a long period of time? Are there any remnants of pioneering species still around; for example, old "overmature" aspen trees? (You will have to look closely because the familiar silver-green bark of the young aspen becomes dark and deeply furrowed in old age.) Are the saplings in the understory of the same species as the overstory trees, or will the site someday belong to another species, perhaps even the conifers?

If the forest is not multistoried, are the trees all approximately the same size, suggesting an even-aged stand that might have started with widespread disturbance? Are there any old stumps that suggest a clear-cutting operation, or old blowdowns to suggest wind damage to the former stand? Is there any evidence of fire, such as bits of charcoal lying on top of the mineral soil or charred stumps and logs? Do the overstory species themselves suggest the nature of disturbance? Extensive stands of paper birch sometimes follow a burn. Yellow birch and pin cherry often crop up in lines where the mineral soil has been exposed by old skid trails.

And while you are hiking in these forests, look for "bear trees." Black bears are crazy about beech nuts, and when they climb beech trees to forage they leave claw marks on the smooth gray bark that callous over and remain visible for years.

TREES FROM THE WAIST DOWN

If you are at all like me, you often cover many miles of trail laboring under a heavy pack and looking at your feet. This doesn't mean that you have to hike with blinders, though, sacrificing all that's happening along the way just to stay on schedule. It's quite easy, in fact, to keep track of how the forest changes as you walk; you need only know how to identify trees without looking up. For your hiking pleasure, then, here are a few trees that are easy to identify from the waist down that can serve as useful indicators of successional or elevational change.

## *Smooth-Barked Trees*

SMOOTHNESS IS a relative term. But in the words of Richard Smyth, a naturalist friend of mine, "If you imagine yourself shinnying down a tree with shorts on, then it becomes quite easy to separate the smooth from the rough."

AMERICAN BEECH
*A hard, smooth bark, tight and nonflaking, with numerous raised "freckles." The trunks and branches of beech are always a "cool" light gray (almost bluish), resembling elephant skin.*

BALSAM FIR

*Slightly rougher and a darker gray than beech, flaking a little, with numerous pitch blisters that break easily when pressed (a warty elephant skin).*

QUAKING ASPEN

*Conspicuous light gray-green color. The bark of older trees becomes rough and furrowed on the lower half of the trunk, but the characteristic smooth greenish bark can always be seen in the upper parts of the tree.*

STRIPED OR GOOSEFOOT MAPLE

*Prominent narrow, vertical white stripes on the smooth greenish bark of young trees gives this species one of its common names. As the tree ages, the bark turns reddish, with less conspicuous striping. This small tree rarely reaches over 8 inches in diameter.*

WHITE ASH

*Soft, tight, nonscaly bark, finely fissured in a diamondlike pattern, particularly on older trees. Medium gray in color, this bark has a unique texture to it, like the checkering on a gunstock, that is easy to recognize at a distance.*

PIN CHERRY

*Dark reddish brown when young, tending toward charcoal gray as the tree matures. An almost lustrous bark with numerous and prominent horizontal lenticels.*

MOUNTAIN ASH

*Some resemblance to pin cherry, but lighter in color, and lenticels raised more, sometimes coalescing into horizontal bands. This high-elevation tree is not likely to be found alongside pin cherry.*

YELLOW BIRCH

*Golden or sometimes silvery bark, peeling in thin narrow curls with lenticels forming conspicuous horizontal streaks. Very old trees develop rough, scaly bark, but branches and roots still show the smooth gold color. Twigs have a nice wintergreen flavor.*

PAPER BIRCH

*White to tawny (sometimes even pinkish or orange) on mature tree, with bark peeling in wide strips. Young trees, particularly at high elevation, often have dark reddish and unpeeling bark with prominent thin white lenticels. Twigs lack the wintergreen flavor of yellow birch.*

GRAY BIRCH

*Tight, unpeeling white bark with numerous black markings, giving it a dirty look. Black, triangular patches ("Chinese beards") beneath branches are prominent. This species occasionally hybridizes with paper birch and shows some of the characteristics of both.*

## *Rough-Barked Trees*

AGAIN THIS IS a subjective category, but if you were shinnying with shorts on, these trees would hurt.

SUGAR AND RED MAPLES

*These two start out with smooth gray bark, although the red maple has a colder, steely gray bark similar to beech (look at the buds to quickly tell the difference in winter), while the sugar maple has a warmer brownish gray bark, often with many "silver dollar" patches of lichens. As the trees age, however, the bark becomes deeply furrowed and flaking; this distinguishes the trees as maples but offers no fail-safe way to tell the two species apart.*

BLACK CHERRY

*Dark bark, chocolate brown to black, scaling and curling outward to give a very rough appearance. Breaking off a curl and smelling it will reveal the pungent odor characteristic of cherry.*

RED SPRUCE

*Dark, coarse bark, broken into plates or scales of irregular size and shape. The bark exudes sticky, light-colored gum deposits that some people like to chew.*

HEMLOCK

*Medium to dark brown bark, scaly in young trees, but becoming deeply furrowed with age, not resembling any of the other conifers in our woods.*

WHITE PINE

*Smooth and conspicuously dark greenish-gray bark on young trees. The bark begins to crack with age, however, especially around the branches (only the oldest trees become deeply furrowed like hemlocks). The branches are whorled, radiating out from the trunk like spokes on a wagon wheel.*

III.

# Pattern and Adaptation at High Elevation

At elevations above 2500 feet the hardwood forest undergoes a rapid transition and climbing farther is like a fast trip north. The changes seen over the next 1000 vertical feet mimic those that would be seen by driving several hundred miles farther north. Already the red maple, black cherry, white ash, and hemlock of the lower hardwood association have disappeared, and the beech is dropping out quickly. Sugar maple is dwindling in numbers too, and yellow birch is beginning to give way to more and more paper birch. The red spruce that comprised a minor part of the lower hardwood forests is beginning to grow more thickly now, and mountain ash, a faithful indicator of the changes to come at still higher elevations, has already made its appearance here and there. The forest is starting to take on a more northern character.

These changes are not a response to increasing elevation *per se*—that is, trees do not respond directly to a reduction in atmospheric pressure. Rather, they are a response to the decrease in temperature, with its myriad of physical and biological effects, that goes along with the elevational change. As noted in Chapter I, on the average, air and soil temperatures decrease by about 3 degrees F for every 1000-foot increase in elevation in the Northeast's mountains, and along with this decrease goes an increase in precipitation of about 8 inches annually per 1000 feet, all of which has a telling influence on tree growth.

The most obvious effect of lower temperatures is a reduction of chemical and biological reaction rates that slows all life processes, even for organisms adapted to growing in cold places. Plants sometimes show a remarkable ability to adjust to temperature changes—balsam fir at high elevation, for example, carries out photosynthesis more efficiently at low temperatures than does balsam fir in the valleys. But by and large, the rate of photosynthesis and the conversion of carbohydrates into new tissues is much reduced at high elevations. And low temperatures also have an important influence on the development of soils at high elevation which further affects tree growth. Slower chemical reactions mean reduced weathering of rock and slower release of mineral nutrients, and reduced microbial activity in the colder soils means slower decomposition and nutrient turnover, creating a bottleneck in the circulation of materials within the forest ecosystem. On top of these conditions, the increased precipitation at higher elevations, while it contributes some nutrients to the soil, also leaches the soil of its more soluble elements and carries them down into the lower forests, leaving the higher forests nutrient poor. At elevation, then, is where the evergreen advantage begins to show.

The transition from hardwood to boreal forest is a surprisingly abrupt one. By 3000 feet the only remnants of the hardwood forest are an occasional yellow birch and a

## NONCONFORMISTS IN THE BOREAL FOREST

*As the deciduous hardwood trees extend their ranges farther north or higher into the mountains, they experience still shorter growing seasons, eventually reaching their limits where the tree can produce only enough photosynthate during the summer to cover its year-round maintenance needs. From this point on, colonization is a losing proposition and the hardwoods give way to the more conservative and tolerant conifers. The exceptions are always noteworthy, and one has to marvel at the ability of paper birch and aspen to grow all the way to the arctic treeline and of paper birch to grow to the northern Appalachians' treeline also. These trees are competing against an evergreen strategy that is undisputably successful throughout the far northern boreal forest, and it's fun to speculate about how they manage it.*

*One possibility is that limited photosynthetic activity in bark tissues supplements the photosynthesis in the leaves. It would be no surprise to find substantial amounts of chlorophyll in the very green bark of aspen, but it so happens that paper birch also has a good amount of chlorophyll in its inner bark, as do many other deciduous species. And some photosynthesis has been measured in twigs of a number of different species immediately after a thaw in midwinter. It is tempting to suggest that aspen and birch survive in the far north by complementing stores from their efficient summer leaves with at least occasional bark photosynthesis during the warmer days of winter. The same may also be true of tamarack, the only deciduous conifer found in the North Woods. While bark photosynthesis may account for only a small percentage of a tree's overall annual carbohydrate gains, any opportunity to offset the continual drain of energy reserves that occurs through respiration during the winter would seem to be of adaptive value.*

few understory herbs and shrubs—like wood sorrel, shining club moss, clintonia, and hobblebush—that make it through the transition. Balsam fir increases in numbers and the forest closes in. We are now in the subalpine spruce-fir zone.

These subalpine forests are built on an old felsenmeer ("sea of rock") substrate: frost-shattered rock left over from a period of intense cold after the summits of these mountains had been cleared by glaciers (*Figure 13*). Water that seeped into the cracks of the freshly exposed bedrock froze and expanded and with a force of 150 tons per square foot wedged the rock apart and broke it into a rubble of sharp, angular fragments very different from the smoothly rounded boulders and cobbles left in the lowlands. On this rock pile the northern Appalachians'

FIGURE 13 *Trail erosion reveals the nature of the northern Appalachians' subalpine forest soils. This angular rock, so familiar to hikers in the Northeast's mountains, is a product of intense frost wedging that took place after deglaciation. Trees anchored among these rocks often experience excessive root abrasion as they sway in the wind.*

FIGURE 14 *Windthrow and breakage are common in the subalpine forest, where spruce and fir are shallow rooted and subjected to high winds and heavy accumulations of rime ice or snow. Damage of this nature is occasionally concentrated in small areas but should not be confused with bands of wave mortality where trees die before they are blown over (compare with Figure 17).*

subalpine forests perch with their roots probing among the pockets and crevices for a grip. And sometimes their grip is only tentative. When the wind blows hard you can often feel the ground move underfoot as roots are wrenched and scraped and broken. In places the trees are tossed randomly about, one across another, under high winds or heavy snow loads (*Figure 14*); and in this cold forest where decomposition is so slow, they lie so for decades, a deterrent to even the most determined off-trail hikers.

Covering this rocky substrate is a thick forest floor of organic matter. Spruce and fir seem to have little problem regenerating here and in places grow so densely that scarcely any light reaches the ground beneath them. If there is any ground cover at all it is likely to be a carpet of haircap moss and a miniature understory of wood sorrel mixed with goldthread, bunchberry, and the single leaves of sterile Canada mayflower—all evergreen herbs. And if it is wet, sphagnum moss may provide the only ground cover. Where there is a little more light, spinulose wood fern grows thickly along with wood asters and clintonia. And of course along the trailside or where a tree has been uprooted to expose mineral soil, we find a variety of plants typical of the higher elevations—currant, mountain ash, paper birch—but elsewhere, late-lying snow and frequent June frosts limit most other species.

## *Dealing with Disturbance*

ALL THESE FEATURES change dramatically with disturbance, and disturbance is an important aspect of the northern Appalachians' subalpine forest ecosystems. As we have already seen, windthrow is common on these rocky soils, and in a moment we will see how wind exposure leads to another form of cyclic dieback that periodically opens up the forest. Even the very deep snow cover that accumulates on the higher slopes helps shape these subalpine forests. The slow but inexorable creep of

LICHENS

*Nothing contributes so much to the far north feeling in our spruce-fir forests as do the lichens that drape the branches and trunks of weathered conifers. Lichens, in fact, exemplify plant adaptation to the rigors of the boreal forest and the tundra beyond.*

*These lichens are not parasitic organisms relying on their host for sustenance: rather they are free-living plants using the tree solely for mechanical support and as a means to obtain more sunlight than is available on the forest floor. Lichens are actually*

*composed of two distinctly different plant forms, an alga and a fungus, growing together where neither is able to succeed alone. The fungal partner is basically a decomposer organism by design. It produces no chlorophyll and, when not associated with algae, obtains its energy from the breakdown of dead organic matter. In the lichen association, however, the fungus derives considerable benefit by harboring photosynthetic algal cells that transfer sugars from their own chlorophyllous tissues to the fungus. From this vantage point, the fungus seems to be the one benefiting most from the association and actually regulates, even suppresses, the growth of the algal cells in a kind of controlled parasitism. The relationship is not entirely one-sided, however, as the algal cells benefit both from the mechanical protection provided by the fungal body and from the nutrients absorbed by fungal hyphae (the equivalent of roots). For this reason, lichens are usually cited as an example of true symbiosis.*

*The question of whether or not one partner benefits more than the other in this relationship is only academic, for the combination of life forms in a single organism is remarkably successful under the harshest of conditions. Lichens are resistant to extreme low temperatures and able in some cases to photosynthesize at*

*Old Man's Beard Lichen*

*below-freezing temperatures. They can withstand extended droughts (lichens are common in hot deserts as well as polar ones) and then "revive" instantly by absorbing water directly into their photosynthetic tissues, unencumbered by a vascular conducting system that must continually repair itself to remain functional. And they are able to extract nutrients where there is no soil at all, chemically etching the surface of bare rock for scarce minerals or straining water as it drips down the branches of a tree. Lichens are indeed the foremost pioneers of the plant world, but ironically, many of them have little resistance to the pollutants of our technological world, especially sulfur dioxide, and some species have disappeared entirely from areas affected by even low level industrial emissions.*

snow downhill under the weight of several accumulated feet puts constant pressure on the trees, causing them to grow asymmetrically, with "pistol butt" bases arching upward from the sloping ground. You can often tell how deep the snow lies on these slopes by noticing the lichen growth on the trunks of the trees. Because lichens require relatively high light levels and grow best above the snowpack, a "lichen line" is often visible on the trees, indicating the normal snow depth (*Figure 15*). And where slopes are especially steep, the snowpack periodically slips, sending an avalanche roaring down the mountainside, a wide swath of broken trees in its wake. In some of the steep-sided ravines on the leeward sides of ridges in the White Mountains, like Tuckerman and Huntington ravines on Mount Washington, avalanches occur repeatedly along the same course, their tracks marked by the dense growth of mountain alder and shrubby paper birch, whose oblique stems lie pressed to the ground under the weight of snow during much of the year (*Figure 16*). And landslides, too, occasionally open a swath through the subalpine forest, allowing colonization of the soil by species

FIGURE 15 *Lichens that encrust the bark of spruce and fir in the subalpine forest are not as abundant on the lower part of the tree trunk because of the diminished light under late-lying snow cover. The dark bases of these fir trees thus indicate the average annual snow depth—about 5 feet in this stand.*

FIGURE 16 *Repeated avalanches along the same path leave telltale "tracks" where only mountain alder and stunted paper birch saplings are able to grow. In this photograph of the Tuckerman Ravine headwall on the east side of Mount Washington, the darker foliage of mountain alder outlines such an avalanche track.*

not normally represented in the closed spruce-fir stand.

Higher elevations, where the forest becomes nearly pure fir, exhibit an interesting phenomenon of cyclic disturbance and rejuvenation, a phenomenon that may help explain how these stands came to be nearly pure fir in the first place. Punctuating the dark green ridges of the Adirondack High Peaks region and the northern White Mountains (and to a much lesser extent the Green Mountains) are numerous silvery, often crescent-shaped bands of dying trees. These bands are found on the more wind-exposed slopes and are usually oriented in the same direction, often in rows, as if controlled by some underlying structure. Many of our hiking trails intersect these dieback areas, and when we walk through them we often pass them off as blowdown. But they result from a much more dynamic process than random blowdown, and when we look closely at these areas we notice that in fact the trees are standing dead, having died on their feet long before their bare trunks were to be toppled by the wind.

These dieback zones are part of a "fir wave," and so far as is known, they occur in just two parts of the world—the northern Appalachian Mountain chain and the mountains of Japan (*Figure 17*). Fir waves are moving bands of death and regeneration that advance systematically through mature forest stands at a rate of 3 to 10 feet per year. Nearly everything in the path of these waves succumbs, while fir, almost exclusively, regenerates in their wake. This configuration gives the forest a wavelike profile: just behind the advancing dieback zone tree height abruptly decreases, but with greater distance from the dieback, trees become progressively older and taller, until the wave "crests" with another dieback zone and more sapling regeneration behind it. The distance between two successive wave fronts varies with the rate of movement and the age of the forest stand, but it averages around 200 feet, with a repeat time of sixty to seventy

A.

FIGURE 17 *"Fir waves" are moving bands of dying trees, shown here in profile on a ridge top (a) and advancing uphill into a mature stand on a lower slope (b). Note in the lower photo that the trees along the leading edge are standing dead, not simply windthrown. Such cyclic disturbance is common in the northern Appalachians and in the mountains of Japan.*

B.

years. These waves can move upslope or downslope, but they always progress in the direction of the prevailing wind, and the end of the wave always comes when it passes over the crest of a ridge.

The death of trees occurs fairly rapidly in a fir wave and results from an accumulation of stresses over time. Forest stands in wave-prone areas are basically even aged—the trees all start together when the overstory opens up and fir regenerates abundantly. While the trees are saplings, growing conditions are not too bad. The young trees are reasonably sheltered and have ample moisture, and as light floods the forest floor they grow vigorously. But with stand densities sometimes exceeding five thousand trees per acre, the competition for scarce resources soon becomes intense. Reaching for sunlight under increasingly crowded conditions, the trees grow lean, lower branches get shaded out, and with time, the amount of foliage relative to the increasing mass of the tree diminishes. The trees must compete for everything now, and as they race for light they grow with virtually no taper at all, eventually to a height of 25 or 30 feet. As the trees outgrow their shelter they become precariously balanced on the thin mantle of soil, and they lean on each other for support as they increasingly suffer mechanical stresses.

When the trees were young and vigorous, they produced photosynthate in excess of their maintenance needs and so had surplus energy reserves to deal with problems of mechanical injury, like tissue repair and replacement. But now that the trees are larger and have more living tissue in roots, trunk, and crown to provide for, their respiration costs are far greater, and the tree is no longer able to produce photosynthate in excess of what is needed to maintain itself. The trees also have reached a height where they suffer greater pressure from the wind and from heavy accumulations of rime ice that collects as cold clouds sweep across the mountain slopes (see the box on page 100). The weather-beaten trees begin to lose productive foliage and soon are barely breaking even in terms of meeting their maintenance needs. If a single tree goes down now and opens up a small gap in the canopy, the force of the wind at the exposed canopy edge increases and the trees situated along the downwind side of the gap lose still more foliage. The trees begin to sway more in the wind, rocking back and forth on the shallow substrate, and their root systems suffer considerable abrasive damage, which adds to their problems. Fungi in the soil that normally make their living by decomposing dead organic matter move into the wounded root tissues and begin to parasitize the tree, tapping it for carbohydrates and placing still more demand on limited photosynthetic reserves. The tree responds to this injury by taking the root out of service but often overreacts, closing off more root tissue than was actually damaged. So now the tree is under duress at both ends, losing foliage and roots at an accelerated pace, and in an environment where growing conditions may be marginal to begin with, the loss is just too great. The tree eventually dies by attrition. The opening in the canopy grows larger, the process of death is repeated along the exposed edge, and a fir wave is born.

To the individual tree the result is, of course, disastrous. To the aging forest as a whole, however, the process has a more positive effect. Nutrients that have been tied up for decades in the wood of the tree are released again, sunlight reaches the understory once more, and for a while the forest will be young and vigorous. We see these fir waves now as an important mechanism in the cyclic renewal of the Northeast's subalpine forests, which are too moist for the fires and too cold for the insect outbreaks that would otherwise periodically rejuvenate an aging forest.

RIME ICE

*The winds that sculpture trees at high elevations display an element of artistry that renders ample reward to those who make a summit climb in subfreezing conditions. Few of nature's weather tricks are as impressive as the feather work of rime ice on trees and rocks that protrude into the cloud stream on a cold day.*

*Rime ice forms when clouds swept by high winds across the mountainside in cold weather leave frozen droplets on anything exposed. The water droplets in the cloud are very small, and because their surface tension is so high, they resist freezing and remain liquid at temperatures well below the freezing point of water—even down to −40 degrees F. But this "supercooled"*

*state is a very tenuous one, and impact with any cold object results in instantaneous crystallization of the water droplet. As the cloud sweeps past a tree, then, ice builds up on the windward side of every branch and every needle, growing in thickness as one tiny cloud droplet after another hits and freezes. If the wind is very strong and steady from one direction, ice will build outward in thin feathery vanes pointing into the wind and creating an ice sculpture of incomparable detail.*

*For all its intricate beauty, though, rime ice can wreak havoc with an evergreen conifer. As winds shift, the ice-encrusted foliage of the conifer is sent sailing away, and along with it goes much of the promise of another growing season. In subalpine fir forests, up to one-fifth of the foliage of trees exposed to wind at the edge of canopy gaps may come down during the winter as a result of this ice loading—a loss from which some trees never recover.*

## *The Limits to Tree Growth*

A FEW YEARS ago I happened to be up on Franconia Ridge in the White Mountains when a trail crew from the Appalachian Mountain Club was reconstructing parts of the Appalachian Trail. I remember watching a crew member digging a trench across the trail for a waterbar and I remember thinking at the time how deep the mineral soil was at that particular spot and how it got to be that way. And I wondered then why the soil did not support the growth of trees in place of the healthy sedge turf of its alpine lawn, for just 50 feet away and not 10 feet lower in elevation, the impenetrable thickets of balsam fir and black spruce ended abruptly, and the low-growing herbaceous sedges and rushes took over from there (*Figure 18*). I had only recently finished three win-

FIGURE 18 *Balsam fir krummholz growing in an alpine meadow on Mount Lafayette, New Hampshire. Only a short distance away, and barely 10 feet lower in elevation, spruce and fir form the impenetrable edge of the forest—the alpine treeline. What keeps the forest from advancing out into the alpine tundra as this lonely stalwart has?*

ters on Mount Washington researching similar questions about the limits to tree growth as part of my doctoral studies, and here I was still asking why. I knew a few things now that were *not* limiting forest advance at that elevation, but I still had many questions.

The treeline, the edge of the forest as a physiognomic or ecological unit, forms one of the most abrupt and conspicuous boundaries between two different vegetation types to be found anywhere on earth. Crossing the treeline takes you from an environment influenced significantly by biological processes, where the growing climate is modified by the trees themselves, to one in which physical forces dominate—where the plants have very little modifying effect on their environment. And few species, plant or animal, regularly inhabit both sides of the treeline. Even human cultures have evolved separately on one side or the other; in the far north, the arctic treeline forms a distinct boundary between Eskimo cultures adapted to life in the open tundra and woodland Indian cultures adapted to life in the boreal forest. So it is understandable that the causes of treeline and fluctuations in its position over time have attracted the attention of many researchers—climatologists, geographers, and ecologists alike. And given the complexity of treelines worldwide, it is not surprising that the explanations put forth run the gamut from competitive exclusion of forest trees by tundra plants to insufficient carbon dioxide for tree growth at high elevations. What makes generalizations about the cause of treelines difficult is that somewhere in the world there is a good case in support of almost any hypothesis that has ever been presented.

In considering the treeline situation in the northern Appalachians and its possible causes, let's start with the underlying assumption that the forest limit in these mountains is climatically controlled rather than influenced by human activity. This may seem so obvious as to need no mention, but elsewhere in the world human influences have much to do with the nature and position of the treeline, especially where fuel-wood gathering and the grazing of livestock at high elevations are important occupations. Some intriguing place names for some of the Northeast's alpine areas, like the Cow Pasture in the alpine zone on Mount Washington, suggest the possibility of local grazing sometime in the past, but documentation of this kind of activity in the high mountains of the northern Appalachians is lacking. And while these mountains have, as we have seen, had a long history of logging, it is not likely that this activity has left any impression on the present treeline. Pulpwood cutting has occurred at one time or another high into the spruce-fir forests of nearly every mountainside, but the logging of the marginal subalpine forests has never been commercially feasible.

It doesn't appear, either, that tree growth is limited by the absence of suitable substrate at high elevations. While the soils of the alpine zone are generally shallow (my earlier recollection notwithstanding) and low in essential nutrients, these same soils support substantial forest growth at lower elevations, and there is no abrupt change above the treeline in either the nature of these soils or their depth. It seems reasonable, therefore, to assume that the present position and form of the treeline in this region is controlled by some form of interaction between trees and the climate, a likelihood suggested by the very appearance of trees that do manage to grow at the treeline—the stunted, gnarled, and flagged (one-sided) form that we often refer to as krummholz.

The influence of climate on forest development is multifaceted, as we have noted, and limitations at the forest edge may involve restrictions at any phase in a tree's growth and development. One of the more widely accepted notions about the cause of treeline is that trees at the forest edge commonly suffer death by desiccation. This is assumed to be a particularly acute problem during winter, when the water lost from foliage exposed to the sun and wind cannot be replaced because the soil is frozen. In some treeline areas of the world, this condition is no doubt a severe limitation, and where excessive winter water loss is a problem, it is usually tied to incomplete maturation of needles, in particular of their protective waxy cuticle, during a short, cool growing season. But winter desiccation does not seem to be much of a problem in the northern Appalachians, partly because wind, surprisingly enough, is not the true culprit when it comes to water loss from a dormant tree. The real problem arises when foliage exposed to intense solar radiation above the snowpack, while sheltered from the wind, heats up as much as 25 or 30 degrees F above air temperature. Heating the leaf drives water out of it, and if the exposed foliage is thawed while the rest of the tree remains frozen, the result is invariably damaging water loss. But this desiccation does not happen under cloud cover or when the wind is blowing, two conditions that seem to prevail throughout the winter at the treeline in the Northeast. When a tree is exposed to strong sunlight above the snow cover, even a slight increase in windspeed helps the plant by dissipating the excess heat and reducing, rather than increasing, water loss.

This is not to suggest that wind isn't a problem at the treeline, however. To the contrary, whatever ultimately causes the death of upright shoots, it is almost certainly related to wind exposure. A tree sheltered in the lee of a rock will usually do very well until it outgrows its protection, and then, if the leader survives at all, its branches become strongly flagged to one side as the various actions of the wind shape the tree. Very often we see balsam fir and red spruce at the treeline producing multiple upright leaders that repeatedly die back while the lateral branches close to the ground fare much better, producing a dense cluster of basal foliage (*Figure 19*). Sometimes the tree is so perfectly trimmed as to show very graphically the flow of wind over a protective ridge or large rock. A distinction should be made here, though, between wind "training," where branches subjected to a steady force on the windward side are trained to grow around to the leeward side, and storm "pruning," where branches on the windward side suffer death by one cause or another and are eventually broken off by high winds. Most flagging at the treeline results from the latter, while trees exposed on lower slopes where wind is intensified along the valley bottom are often trained.

A common form of wind damage in the northern Appalachians is abrasion by wind-carried ice particles. Like

FIGURE 19 *The environment close to the ground sustains healthy foliage on this balsam fir at the treeline. As the tree produces upright leaders, however, exposure to high winds and lower temperatures continually kills them back. The success of lower branches in this case relates to a combination of warmer temperatures near the ground during the growing season and protection under the snowpack from wind damage during winter.*

sand blowing across a beach dune, ice grains whipping over the snowpack have tremendous abrasive power against the relatively soft tissues of exposed trees. Bark on the windward sides of exposed trunks is sometimes abraded right to the wood, and within that zone of maximum transport just above the surface of the snow, foliage may be stripped away entirely. And once needles are broken off, desiccating water loss may follow.

Apart from the obvious physical damage, this loss of photosynthetic tissue is critical under marginal growing conditions, as we saw in fir waves at slightly lower elevations. These needles begin photosynthesis early in the spring, building up reserve energy that contributes substantially to the tree's growth before new needles begin to pay back their own costs, and the loss of these overwintering needles may never be recovered. If the terminal buds somehow survive this peril each winter, and if summer growing conditions are favorable, the tree may eventually reach above the zone of abrasion to maintain a "mop head" of foliage at the top of a bare trunk, a growth habit known as broomsticking (*Figure 20*). But the struggle for a tenuous position is difficult; success in this case often brings on other problems like increased encrustation by rime ice, which is likely to break off in the wind, taking foliage with it.

The most successful tree species at the treeline is the prostrate mat form of black spruce (*Figure 21*). This spe-

FIGURE 20 *Ice particles whipped by high winds on the Lion's Head, Mount Washington, strip branches of foliage during the winter. The growth of surviving buds, supported by carbohydrate from needles left on the lower branches, may eventually elevate the crown above the zone of maximum abrasion, producing a "mop head" of foliage.*

FIGURE 21 *Black spruce shows remarkable genetic flexibility that often allows it to grow entirely prostrate above the treeline. Clonal islands like this one spread by means of adventitious roots (roots that develop from branches), exploiting a much warmer microclimate and avoiding entirely the problems of ice blast during winter.*

cies has the genetic flexibility to change its growth habit according to the demands of its environment, and can spread by means of adventitious roots (roots that develop from branches). Thus the black spruce grows in a mat, without ever attempting to produce an upright leader. The mats show little evidence of physical damage, as they remain protected under the snowpack during most of the winter. But, in addition, by growing along the ground instead of upright, these trees are exploiting a much warmer microclimate, which highlights another important aspect of wind exposure—its effect on plant temperatures during the summer. When the snow cover is gone, both the ground and the plant foliage provide a dark surface that absorbs incoming solar radiation and heats up, warming the air close to the ground. While wind might easily dissipate this heat, wind speed drops off sharply near the ground, so the closer the plant grows to the ground, the warmer it is—an obvious advantage during the growing season. Thus "protection," as we have used the word, may mean freedom from physical abuse, or it may mean a more favorable thermal environment through reduction of wind speed. In most cases it is likely a combination of the two.

Survival and growth are not the only considerations at any treeline; if the forest is to maintain itself or advance into the tundra, successful reproduction is also required. Whether or not this poses a serious limitation at the treeline in the Northeast is a little difficult to establish. Black spruce at the treeline produces infrequent cone crops, and the seeds often are incompletely developed. But a tree that produces a successful seed crop only once or twice in a century can establish enough seedlings to keep a stand going, and black spruce also reproduces vegetatively, as was noted earlier. Balsam fir, on the other hand, produces cone crops more frequently, and this species is at least occasionally successful in establishing seedlings at the treeline. On Mount Washington, for instance, a winter road above the treeline is used occasionally by maintenance crews driving tracked vehicles, and here, where the normal cover of tundra vegetation is very sparse, the edges of the trail sometimes look like seedbeds, with numerous established fir seedlings. So it appears that fir can reproduce at the treeline under favorable site conditions, although opportunities for seedlings to establish themselves amid the undisturbed tundra vegetation are limited. And even if seed germinates and begins to grow successfully in a protected location, the seedling's chance of surviving the physical rigors of the treeline environment when it grows out of the protection of a sheltering rock or other trees is quite another matter.

Conditions above the treeline are probably not limiting enough to prevent a tree from growing, in terms of that function alone. When we analyze the growth rings of a tree at the forest limit, we find that while annual increments are very narrow, the tree always adds some wood, which is evidence that the tree is producing enough photosynthate to satisfy its basic needs. The allocation of carbohydrate among the various tissues and growth functions is prioritized, and wood is generally lowest on the list, so that if there is not enough carbohydrate to go around, wood production is dropped. A tree might produce wood for competitive reasons, but no physiological reasons make it necessary every year. For example, when growing under severe drought stress, trees in the Southwest may fail to produce wood during many growing seasons but live on for centuries. So while growth is very much reduced at the treeline, it is apparently sufficient for the tree to maintain itself in the absence of other physiological constraints.

The problem here, though, seems to be too little "profit margin" during the summer to cover wintertime losses. Abrasive damage by wind-carried ice particles and rime-ice encrustation can remove as much foliage from branches exposed above the snowpack as was produced the previous year (*Figure 22*). Maintaining such a precarious balance between leaf gains and losses in this environment will never suffice because as production of woody tissues continues, respiration requirements may increase until a compensation point is reached and the annual carbohydrate budget of the tree is no longer balanced. Some part of the tree will then die. So the relatively low timberline in the northern Appalachians seems best explained in terms of the suppression of photosynthetic production coupled with heavy annual loss of leaf and shoot tissues owing to high winds.

FIGURE 22 *Time-lapse photographs of a balsam fir at the treeline on Mount Washington, New Hampshire. The photo on the right was taken four years after the photo on the left. By comparing individual branches it can be seen that the tree has been producing substantial new growth each summer but that most of it is stripped away during the winter. Such a close balance between gains and losses in an environment so rigorous puts the tree in a very tenuous position.*

## *Life in High Places*

TREES AT THE forest limit may have trouble balancing their carbon budgets, but the low-growing shrubs and herbs in the tundra beyond have found the secret. In this most limiting of mountain environments, miniaturization seems to be the answer. Dwarf willows, birches, and heath shrubs may grow upright in the protected hollows among rocks; but elsewhere they sprawl, like the prostrate black spruce at the treeline, flat on the ground seeking a warmer microclimate—that thin protective zone where the wind does not hit as hard and the air is warmed by the soil's absorption of solar radiation (*Figure 23*). Other plants do the same. The mountain sandwort that often lines the trails above the treeline grows in small tufts barely an inch in height, with narrow leaves loosely interwoven to trap the precious warmth at ground level. Diapensia grows in such a compact "cushion" that it creates its own self-sustaining microenvironment, its tightly packed leaves, almost impervious to the wind, and the organic soil that accumulates beneath the dark, absorbing foliage often is several degrees warmer than the surrounding air. Thus the common theme in the alpine tundra is staying small and low to the ground to make the most of the advantages gained by absorbing sunlight. Here permanence takes on a new dimension. It is no longer a matter of adding support tissue every year to hold the plant up, for this game is won not by mechanical strength but by subtle, often invisible strategies—internal physiological adjustments to match the outward physical modifications. And the small size of these plants keeps maintenance needs to a minimum, helping substantially to balance the carbohydrate budget of each plant in an energy-deficient environment.

That such morphological characteristics in alpine veg-

DIAPENSIA

A.

FIGURE 23 *Genetically dwarfed willows above the treeline (a) are "programmed" to grow prostrate along the ground, where they take advantage of the sun's warmth absorbed by the underlying rock or soil. Miniature rhododendrons with large showy blossoms (b) also hug the rocks, exploiting the only microclimate—those few inches above the ground—where life is possible in the alpine zone.*

B.

MOUNTAIN SANDWORT

etation have emerged so universally through genetic trial and error is not surprising in light of the nature of alpine environments everywhere. To be sure, calm days occur on the high summits when the brilliance of the sun is unmatched anywhere else, and they too are part of the weather complex to which alpine plants must remain sensitive. But the frequent summit visitor knows too well that the opposite extreme is more often the case: the Northeast's alpine areas are frequently shrouded in clouds, pummeled for days at a time by high winds, and subjected to snow and freezing temperatures during any month of the growing season. Consider for a minute that on Mount Washington in New Hampshire, cloud cover obscures the summit 55 percent of the time; the wind blows 35 miles per hour on the average, day and night, with hurricanes of 70 miles per hour or greater occurring during every month of the year (the wind speed of 231 miles per hour on Mount Washington is still the land record!); and the highest temperature ever recorded at the Mount Washington Observatory was only 72 degrees F.

Mount Washington is the extreme, of course, but weather records collected at other high-elevation stations like Mount Mansfield in Vermont and Whiteface Mountain in the Adirondacks tell the same story: conditions in the alpine zone are cold and windy throughout the growing season. It is primarily to these conditions that the plants must adapt. Survival during winter is not enough, for alpine plants must also be able to grow and reproduce at the low temperatures of summer, and they are superbly adapted to doing so.

In an environment dominated by physical forces, where the plants themselves exert little influence on growing conditions, we might expect to see a fairly homogeneous vegetation cover—a single alpine community adapted to a common set of environmental constraints. But such is not the case, for even here we find plants varying in their tolerances, and seemingly small differences in topography and microclimate can make a big difference in the distribution of species (*Figure 24*). The highland rush, a number of different sedges, and the heath shrubs dominate the alpine vegetation, and they differ from one another in their response to temperature, their requirements for soil moisture, and their tolerance of late-lying snow cover. Thus they form different communities recognizable by the relative proportions of each species. On the coldest slopes, especially north- and west-facing exposures with frequent fog and high soil

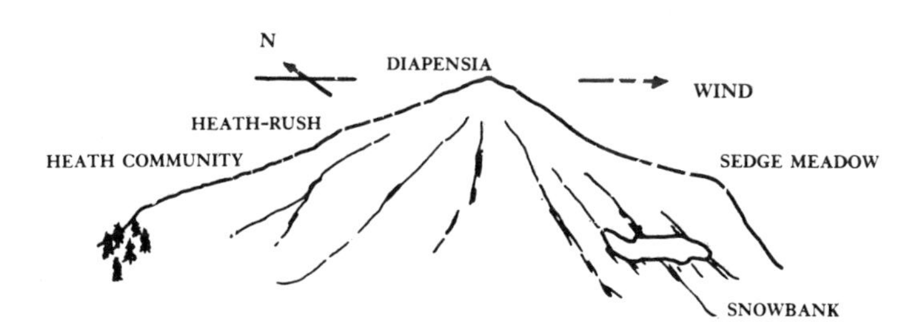


FIGURE 24 *Distribution of plant communities in the alpine zone of the northern Appalachian Mountains. The dominant alpine species distribute themselves along topographic gradients according to specific tolerances or requirements for temperature, soil moisture, or snow cover.*

moisture, we find sedge meadows dominating (*Figure 25*). This community is characterized by the abundance of Bigelow's sedge, which produces shoots from underground stems and often forms a dense turf over the rocky substrate. As we move downslope, highland rush and various heath shrubs intermix in an association called (logically) the sedge-heath-rush community. Where drainage is better and snow melts early, the sedge may drop out and the others take over. The heath-rush community so formed is often found on south- and east-facing exposures and is dominated by mountain cranberry, alpine bilberry, and, of course, the highland rush. Still further downslope, usually just above the treeline or in protected places where the snow cover is deep but not long lasting, the rush disappears and the heath shrubs dominate. Labrador tea and black crowberry are often

FIGURE 25 *In the upper reaches of the alpine zone, where the slopes are steeped in cloud moisture and the organic soils are continually wet, sedge meadows form the dominant community type. Here, Bigelow's sedge is the most abundant plant species.*

MOUNTAIN CRANBERRY

prominent in this community, along with the other heath shrubs common to the alpine zone.

Two other easily recognizable communities occupy the extremes of snow-cover conditions. Some of the tallest plants to be found in the alpine zone make up the snow-bank community. Species like Indian poke (also known as false hellebore), hairgrass, and alpine goldenrod are found where the snow lies deep and long but where late snow melt provides ample water to support their rapid growth. These snow-bank species are almost always found on the lee sides of our mountains, and because of the protection that such locations afford, herbs from the lower forests sometimes make it into this community. At the opposite end of the spectrum, the diapensia commu-

ALPINE BILBERRY

CROWBERRY

nity, consisting primarily of that species and the very prostrate alpine azalea and Lapland rosebay, flourishes under what would seem the greatest difficulty of all—the most windswept exposures to be found anywhere in the alpine zone. There, where protective snows are continually blown clear, diapensia sometimes persists alone, in frozen solitude throughout the winter (*Figure 26*). Few other species compete successfully under these conditions.

The plants of these alpine communities display many different adaptations, some of which have evolved along parallel lines in very different life forms. The nonvascular lichens and mosses, for example, are very successful in the alpine zone partly because they, like many other species, are able to maintain photosynthetic production at very low temperatures. Some, in fact, continue photosynthetic activity into the winter, having the ability

ALPINE AZALEA

FIGURE 26 *On the most windswept ridges of the high alpine zone, diapensia flourishes, creating its own life-support system beneath a tightly packed envelope of drought-resistant foliage. Where the ground is swept bare of snow cover for much of the winter, few other plant species can compete successfully with diapensia.*

during periods of brief thaw to absorb meltwater directly into their photosynthetic tissues. But the dwarf woody shrubs, whether deciduous or evergreen, have proved equally successful in their respective niches, and so too have the cushion plants, the leafy herbs, and the sedges. The only "rule" that is nearly universal in alpine environments is that the plants, regardless of life form, are perennials. The alpine tundra is no place for annuals—plants that in a single growing season must germinate from seed, grow to maturity, flower, and produce more viable seed to perpetuate the species. The growing season is much too compressed for this habit. While there are a few interesting exceptions in other alpine areas of the world (and their success makes them fascinating objects of study), the alpine communities in the Northeast, as elsewhere, are dominated by perennials.

These perennials assure their own permanence in ways

more reliable than seed production alone. The majority of the vascular plants invest heavily in roots and rhizomes (underground stems), often producing two to ten times as much mass below ground as above. These below-ground organs serve as carbohydrate storage centers to support growth early in the following summer, and it is from them that many plants produce vegetative off-shoots—a common habit in the alpine zone to hedge against the high risk of seed failure. The advantage of vegetative reproduction is its much greater probability of success—a sure start and a genetic make-up identical to the parent's that is already proved in an environment that selects rigorously against the unfit. But vegetative reproduction is a mixed promise. In some respects, the progeny may be too reliant on the parent. The offspring must depend on parental resources for their early development; they are restricted to the parent's site; and perhaps most importantly, they lack the genetic flexibility to adjust to changing environmental conditions. Vegetative reproduction is an ideal way to preserve a genetic makeup that has proved successful, because it prevents the introduction of less favorable genetic traits through cross-fertilization. However, if the environment changes—for instance, if the climate slowly warms or cools or annual precipitation changes in amount or seasonal distribution—then the species may not be able to readapt. Vegetative reproduction, with the constraints of a fixed genetic character, may be an evolutionary deadend.

However, few alpine plants rely on vegetative reproduction alone. Many of these plants, even the species noted for their copious production of vegetative offshoots and their turf-forming ability, sometimes flower prolifically and during a good seed year may produce hundreds of seeds. A patch of mountain sandwort no larger than what your wool hat might cover can yield up to two thousand seeds in a growing season. Diapensia, highland rush, and many other herbs and shrubs are also capable of high seed production. The seeds in these cases are generally viable and often lack any built-in dormancy mechanism, so that they germinate readily as soon as soil temperatures are right for the particular species.

The problems of successful sexual (flowering) reproduction, however, lie not with seed production, but with seed dispersal and seedling establishment. Although it seems counter to our intuition, the high winds of the alpine zone are not especially effective in blowing seeds around. The plants are, after all, of very low stature, and wind speed drops off sharply close to the ground. A study of the natural revegetation of disturbed tundra sites on Franconia Ridge, New Hampshire, found through the use of special seed traps that seeds rarely carried 3 feet from a parent source. Wind may be more effective in transporting seeds across snow and ice, and some plants like diapensia seem to take advantage of this, shaking their seeds out of persistent capsules that poke stiffly above the thin, windswept snow cover. However, dispersal remains a major obstacle in the spread of alpine plants through sexual reproduction, as neither birds, nor rodents, nor rainwaters appear to be any more effective than the wind in getting seeds around.

Once a seed does reach a site suitable for germination,

it must survive forbidding problems of establishment. Especially in the spring and fall, exposed soil surfaces above the treeline undergo wide temperature fluctuation daily, heating up strongly with the absorption of sunlight, but just as rapidly cooling by radiation after sundown. When the soil temperature fluctuates back and forth across the freezing point, the soil surface may pulsate up and down by as much as an inch or more, as water in the soil expands upon freezing and then relaxes again with thawing. This intense frost heaving has a disastrous effect on a tiny seedling. It tears roots apart and pushes the seedling out of the ground before it has a chance to establish itself and stabilize the soil. Alpine plants counter this problem to some extent by very rapid root development in emerging seedlings; they funnel the majority of plant resources into root growth during the first year, then switch to greater above-ground development during the second year. But even so, studies show that on the average only three out of every one hundred germinating seedlings will survive to see a second growing season.

It seems, then, that the best way to perpetuate the species under the constraints of the alpine environment is to combine perennial longevity with the prolific seed output more typically seen in annuals. The 3 percent of the seed population that survives and grows to maturity will maintain some genetic variability in the population, while the year-in and year-out vegetative persistence of the perennial assures survival through bad times.

The distance limitations of vegetative reproduction and the problems of seedling establishment in sexual reproduction can make the colonization of bare soils above the treeline a very slow process. This restriction gives rise to concern over a growing problem in our alpine areas today. Inevitably, the destruction of alpine vegetation follows the ever-increasing numbers of visitors to our high peaks. As more and more of the high ground is laid bare by trampling and subsequent erosion and the below-ground remnants of the former vegetation die off, recovery increasingly depends on successful sexual reproduction. And with the problems that seeds and germinating seedlings face, the establishment of plant cover by this means becomes a game of chance. The odds are best where snow accumulates early and stays late, insulating against rapid and frequent freeze-thaw cycles. Elsewhere the development of a critical mass of plant cover, sufficient to stabilize the site and reduce risk to additional recruits, may come only with a succession of unusually good years. Some predictions, based on the data currently available, put recovery time for many of our disturbed alpine areas at from several decades to a century or more. It is for this reason, perhaps, that custodians of the High Peaks area in the Adirondacks have introduced hardy, nonnative grasses to stabilize badly eroding sites.

Native alpine species, once established, show a remarkable tolerance to the rigors of their environment through a number of physiological adaptations. It should not be surprising, at this point, to learn that these plants in general exhibit a prominent shift in their metabolic response to temperature—that the optimum temperature for numerous metabolic processes is lower in these plants than is the case with herbs and shrubs of more temperate lowland climes. Whereas maximum photosynthetic rates in low-elevation plants may occur at a temperature of 75 to 85 degrees F, in alpine plants photosynthesis may be most efficient at around 55 degrees F. Interestingly, though, because alpine plants often experience wide swings in temperature, they are also adapted to adjusting their photosynthetic rates quickly. Just two or three days of warmer weather can cause these plants to shift their optimum temperature for photosynthesis upward so that they can maximize their photosynthetic opportunity in the short growing season. As a result, photosynthetic rates at any given time in alpine species may be as high as those in lowland plants. Furthermore, alpine plants can convert starch, the primary product of photosynthesis, into sugar and translocate it to other parts of the plant, generally more efficiently at low temperature than can most other plants.

Low temperature is not the only restriction that alpine vegetation has to adjust to. Even the warm sunny days bring their problems at high elevations, for under these conditions plants in the alpine zone are exposed to relatively high levels of ultraviolet radiation. Just as such exposure may cause severe sunburn on our own skin, it can also seriously damage a plant. High doses of ultraviolet radiation cause a number of problems, including the destruction of protein and the breakdown of DNA in the plant. Many plants guard against this danger by producing ultraviolet-absorbing pigments—anthocyanins and flavinoids—in the outer epidermal layers of the leaf (recall that these are the same pigments that give the leaves of some hardwood trees brilliant color in the fall). These pigments serve no function in the photosynthetic process, but alpine plants produce them throughout the season to screen ultraviolet radiation before it reaches the inner mesophyll cells of the leaf, where photosynthesis takes place.

The degree to which alpine plants have adapted to their environment is really quite remarkable. In a physiological sense, they are tough and durable—well equipped to deal with the rigors of the high summits. Yet, with the pressure that growing numbers of hikers are putting on these plant communities, we are continually reminded of the fragility of alpine vegetation. Is there a contradiction here?

It can be argued that no environment is stressful to the organisms that are adapted to it, and such may be the case with alpine vegetation. But tolerance and resilience are two different attributes, and whereas alpine plants exemplify the former, they are quite lacking with regard to the latter. Even though the alpine plant is well adapted to maximizing its growth potential at low temperature, the growing season is, after all, very short and the total plant matter that alpine communities produce in a year is very much less than that for lowland vegetation. And we have seen that getting established initially in this environment is extremely difficult. Although a small number of alpine species—most notably the mountain sandwort—display the characteristics of pioneer species, their effectiveness in colonizing alpine sites is very limited compared to the recovery rates that we see following disturbance in the lowlands. Once soil above the treeline is exposed, its loss of biotic potential tends to accelerate rapidly, further delaying the reestablishment of plant cover on it. In the extreme, the combination of a loss of organic matter, the leaching of nutrients, and an increase in frost heaving leads to the creation of a biological desert. This, too, seems a contradiction, but it is something to think about as we hike in the alpine tundra.

## *Patterns in Stone*

Before leaving this discussion of the alpine environment, we should note some of the interesting topographical features to be found above the treeline, for the same climate that shapes the alpine vegetation also creates a number of unique landscape patterns—circular and linear arrangements of stone—that result from the active movement and sorting of rocks under the influence of ice and gravity. Geomorphologists classify these features as periglacial landforms; the term *periglacial* refers to a climatic situation that is "almost glacial"—cold enough to support seasonal ground-ice formation and frequent freeze-thaw activity, but not cold enough to sustain permanent snow fields or glaciers. The processes at work in the evolution of these landforms require intense freeze-thaw activity, and for this reason periglacial features are best expressed in our highest alpine areas, where snow cover is thin and where frost stirs ground material without being inhibited by tree cover (which reduces the amplitude and frequency of freeze-thaw cycles and restricts soil movement).

Periglacial landforms develop under the influence of three basic processes—frost wedging or shattering, seasonal ground ice formation, and mass movement. Frost wedging is the same process that, after deglaciation, left the rubble of sharp, angular rock on which our subalpine forests perch (*Figure 13*). Water freezing in bedrock joints or in the minute pores of coarsely grained crystalline rock exerts an enormous force that splits the rock into ever smaller pieces, providing a continuous supply of material that may be moved about by subsequent frost heaving. In the simplest case, this frost shattering leads to the development of extensive block fields (the felsenmeer, or "sea of rocks," that we talked about earlier) which may be in constant, although imperceptible downslope motion (*Figure 27a*). On steeper slopes the felsenmeer may align into "block streams," where the local topography funnels the rock into channels resembling stream beds (*Figure 27b*).

The inexorable creep of felsenmeer is encouraged by the freezing of water trapped in the finer materials beneath. As the ice expands, it lifts particles, including the felsenmeer, in a direction perpendicular to the freezing plane (that is, perpendicular to the ground surface), which means that on a slope, the particles are displaced both upward and outward. Upon thawing, they then

A.

FIGURE 27 *Intense frost shattering of bedrock in the alpine zone results in the accumulation of angular fragments on the surface, which are collectively referred to as block fields or felsenmeer (a). As these rocks move slowly downslope, they are sometimes channeled by the local topography into "block streams" (b).*

B.

settle vertically under the influence of gravity, resulting in a net downslope movement of the displaced particles with every freeze-thaw cycle.

Enhancing this process is the development of needle ice in fine-grained soils where an abundant supply of capillary water feeds ice crystals that grow in columns sometimes 3 or 4 inches in height. In bare soils along the trail after the first hard freeze in the fall, needle ice is often seen lifting a cap of soil or rock (*Figure 28*) that will eventually settle downslope from its original position. This downslope creep may also be aided by the flow of saturated soil after thawing, a process known as solifluction.

Freezing activity, whether involving needle ice or not, is also responsible for sorting materials, through the differential rate of movement of large and small particles. A large rock, lifted up by freezing beneath, often cannot

FIGURE 28 *Needle ice forms in fine-textured soils where there is an abundant supply of moisture to feed rapidly growing crystals. The ice grows in a direction perpendicular to the ground plane and is capable of lifting sizable rocks. On a slope, vertical settling after thawing leads to the gradual downslope creep of surface materials.*

settle back down to its original position after the ground thaws because finer particles, stirred by frost action, have filled in the space underneath the rock. Rocks buried in the subsoil are often brought to the surface by this process of ejection, and once on the surface, even the slightest undulations of topography can result in their being moved laterally by creep.

In the alpine zone, where the stirring of soils by frost is particularly intense and uninhibited by tree roots, this sorting process gives rise to a variety of ground patterns including stone circles, garlands, stripes, steps, and terraces. The circles (actually polygons) occur on uneven, but nearly horizontal ground where lateral sorting is active but where there is no sustained downslope movement. Larger particles are moved outward from the centers of hummocks and come to rest in slight hollows or wherever they meet others moving in the opposite direction, thus forming roughly circular netlike patterns under the control of the local topography (*Figure 29a*). Where a slight slope exists, these circles may migrate slowly downhill, opening up to form crescent-shaped garlands. On steeper slopes the garlands may grade into stripes that run parallel to the direction of the slope.

Wherever the efficiency of downslope creep or solifluction changes such that the soil's movement is slowed, a series of steps or terraces may form. This piling up of soil or rock particles may be caused by changes in vegetation, slope, configuration of the underlying bedrock, or any other factor that results in a change in the intensity of freeze-thaw activity. The steps or terraces thus formed (differences between the two being primarily a matter of scale) may be banked either by coarse rock or by vegetation (*Figure 30*).

This simplified discussion belies the complexity of a situation in which many factors act simultaneously on the landscape and any particular class of ground pattern

FIGURE 29 *Frost ejection of subsurface stones followed by their slow lateral creep away from centers of high ground results in the formation of sorted circles or polygons (above). Where the intensity of this action is particularly great, large areas of patterned ground develop (below).*

FIGURE 30 *In areas of active soil movement, terraces may form wherever downslope creep is temporarily slowed, in effect damming the soil or rock particles. In many cases the more protected terrace riser is the only place where plants can establish themselves.*

may have more than one mode of formation. Perhaps the best location in our region for seeing all of these processes at work is in the Alpine Garden and Bigelow Lawn areas of Mount Washington, New Hampshire, where both inactive ("fossil") and presently forming patterns can be found. But anywhere in the alpine regions of the Northeast you might look for patterned ground features, for in this periglacial environment beyond the shelter of the forest, the forces of ice are still paramount in shaping the land.

IV.

# *Epilogue:* The Future of the North Woods

THERE IS A dark cloud hanging over the Northeast's mountains now—a cloud of known chemistry but of only partially understood consequences. We call it acid rain, but it is also acid snow, acid fog, and on a clear day, something the scientific community calls dry deposition. It is atmospheric pollution by any label, a host of gases and particulates released by a multitude of civilized activities—by our refrigerators and air conditioners and aerosol packaging—but mostly, the threatening cloud is nitrogen and sulfur oxides emitted by our power plants and fuel-burning industries; by our home gas, oil, and wood furnaces; and by our automobiles. The bulk of these pollutants are a product of the combustion of fossil fuels, which releases elements tied up for eons in buried and metamorphosed plant remains—a natural cycling process accelerated unfathomably by our technological ingenuity. In effect, every one of our industrial smokestacks is a miniature volcano, injecting these raw elements back into the atmosphere in a fraction of the time that it took to incorporate them into terrestrial ecosystems. And in the atmosphere, these oxides combine with water vapor to form dilute nitric and sulfuric acids in unprecedented quantity.

The chemical reactions that follow when these weak acids combine with other elements are a complicated business. In general, the hydrogen in these acids tends to exchange places with other positively charged elements (like calcium, magnesium, and aluminum) with which they come in contact, in effect "bumping" the positive elements from their site of attachment (on a soil particle, for example) with the result that the replaced element may be leached away in the percolating groundwater and the hydrogen ion left in its place. This is an acidifying process. As we saw in our discussion of sphagnum moss and its role in bog development, this process can and does occur naturally in many instances. Plant roots themselves exchange hydrogen ions for other elements in the active uptake of nutrients and so might also be accused of acidifying the soil. But the problem we face now is one of scale. The increased input of acids from precipitation or atmospheric fallout is in some cases overwhelming the landscape's ability to handle them. If the receiving soils have sufficient calcium or magnesium, for example, to exchange with the hydrogen ions, thus buffering the soil, then the acid deposition may be of little consequence. However, many of our soils are poor in these elements, with the result that aluminum, which is abundant, is exchanged instead. And when the acid goes into the soil and the aluminum comes out, problems occur, for aluminum in solution is toxic to a number of organisms. In the spring, when heavy runoff occurs from snow melt (the snowpack stores nitric and sulfuric acid all winter), we often see a pulse of aluminum in stream water as acids percolate through and overwhelm soils that might normally have some buffering capacity. The aluminum, once in the water, is toxic to fish, interfering with gill respiration and causing death by suffocation. This has been the fate of many aquatic organisms in a great number of lakes in the Adirondack Mountains, where soils are naturally low in buffering capacity.

While we have witnessed the death of lakes and understand the cause, the symptoms of ailing forests have proved much more difficult to diagnose. We know that spruce at high elevations is dying, but the cause remains elusive, complicated by a host of variables including the uncertain effects of short- and long-term climatic fluctuations on forest growth and reproduction. And superimposed on these variables are a number of natural stresses wrought by insects, disease, high winds, and intense competition for limited site resources. We know that each one of these stresses can contribute to tree death, but we also know that a healthy tree is capable of warding off attacking organisms and repairing wounded tissues. The question facing us now is, are the effects of air pollution undermining the vigor and resiliency of our forests?

This is not an easy question to answer. We know that many of the same problems that are plaguing aquatic organisms may also be affecting forest trees. We know, for instance, that aluminum is potentially toxic to plant roots, interfering with root uptake and causing fine-root mortality; but aluminum concentrations are sometimes higher in the roots of healthy trees than in dying ones, and at higher elevations where decomposition is slowed, aluminum binds readily to the more abundant organic matter in the soil, rendering the aluminum unavailable to plants. We know, too, that acid precipitation leaches calcium and other nutrients from the soil, and that a calcium deficiency coupled with higher root concentrations of aluminum can cause root injury. However, at the high elevations where spruce is dying, we more often find the opposite trend to be the case—that calcium/aluminum ratios in roots are greater because as the organic matter in the soil increases with elevation, aluminum availability decreases faster than does calcium availability. We know that acid deposition on the foliage of trees can cause leaching of nutrient cations from the leaf and that in the severest cases, close to the source of industrial emissions, acid deposition can result in erosion of the protective leaf cuticle, leading in turn to plant-water balance problems. However, we do not have any hard evidence that loss of cations from the leaf surface stresses the tree in any way, nor has cuticular erosion been observed in trees that are now suffering the most serious dieback.

This adds a lot of "maybes" to an already complicated situation, but perhaps we can gain some perspective on the matter by looking at the larger picture of trees interacting with their total environment. In doing so, we might find it helpful to place the various stresses that our forest trees face within the conceptual framework suggested by the prominent forest pathologist, Paul Manion, in his book *Tree Disease Concepts* (Prentice-Hall, 1981). In dealing with tree decline syndromes (dieback phenomena, where a clear cause is lacking), such as we are currently witnessing with red spruce at high elevations, Manion groups all stresses into one of three categories as follows:

> *Predisposing factors* are long-term climatic or site factors that weaken a tree growing in an unfavorable location. These factors continually stress the tree, rendering it more susceptible to the actions of other agents.
>
> *Inciting factors* involve short-term actions, either physical or biological, that often produce visible damage to the tree. Counteractive plant response to such injury is inhibited by the effects of predisposing stresses.
>
> *Contributing factors* include those persistent secondary forces that by themselves generally cannot initiate decline

but constantly affect a weakened tree, intensifying the actions of inciting factors.

By categorizing stresses in this manner, we can at least attempt to prioritize some of the problems that we do understand.

Considering the site conditions under which our high-elevation spruce grows, it is easy to understand how these trees might be predisposed to suffer decline under any additional stress placed on them. As we have discussed previously, the low temperatures that prevail at higher elevations affect both photosynthesis and nutrient cycling and uptake rates, and this effect, coupled with intense competition in the very dense subalpine stands, tends to hold the trees closer to their break-even point. As each tree adds biomass, more and more nutrients are sequestered in long-lived woody tissues, leaving less in the soil, while at the same time the increased respiration demands of the tree (more living cells to maintain) leave less photosynthetic reserve to support other needs like tissue repair and production of defense compounds. As we saw at the treeline, living so close to the break-even point is a tenuous position where the balance may be so easily tipped by physical forces like high winds and heavy snow loads. Whereas a tree with ample resources may recover time and time again after mechanical injury—sealing off wounds against invading pathogens, replacing damaged roots with new ones, producing still more foliage to offset losses—a tree at its break-even point, although it may look perfectly healthy, is indeed vulnerable.

When a tree is predisposed to decline, an inciting factor like unusual drought stress or attack by a virulent pathogen will usually cause immediate and visible damage from which the tree (or part of it) is not likely to recover. The destructiveness of the inciting factor, however, may depend on what additional contributing factors are aggravating or compounding the problem. Here, I believe, is where the effects of atmospheric pollution come into the picture. The evidence available so far does not suggest that the varied effects of atmospheric pollution, by themselves, can initiate decline in the tree, except in the extreme case where the tree is located close to the source and receives an exceptionally high dose of pollution. But where the tree's resources for combating stresses are already low and it is besieged by some inciting force, any contributing effect of pollution that causes immobilization or loss of nutrients or interferes with root uptake and translocation will surely hasten the tree's demise. This is not to suggest, however, that these contributing effects might not move up the list to inciting or even predisposing if current trends continue.

There is still much that we don't know. It is too early, for example, to measure the effects of heavy metals like lead, which have accumulated to alarming levels in our high-elevation soils, on litter decomposition and nutrient cycling—processes that if disrupted, will affect the whole ecosystem with time. Short-term studies suggest that current levels of lead are not sufficient to cause a reduction in decomposition rates, but we know too well that lead is toxic to many biological systems and that it is extremely persistent in the environment. So the jury is still out on this and many other issues, and is likely to be so for some time to come.

But is it not enough to know that acid deposition may be a contributing factor in the decline of some forest ecosystems, if not a predisposing or inciting one? Do we need to convict it in the first degree before doing something about it? We can see that the levels of pollution now intercepted by our forests are inimical to some organisms at different levels in their physiology or life cycle, ultimately reducing photosynthetic capacity or reproductive output. Do we need to wait for the next phase of ecosystem degradation, where species are lost or cease to become functional members of the forest community, before we take action? We expect a lot from our forests now. We look to them for fuel, for wood products, for food, and in increasing instances, we look to them to take care of our wastes—to absorb and purify human effluent as we spray it onto the hillsides surrounding our mountain resorts. And all this our forests can do if we do not overburden them—if we temper our expectations with the realization that these wonderfully complex and efficient ecosystems have a finite capacity for abuse. We have seen that our forests are remarkably resilient under ordinary circumstances, but we must not push them beyond their limits, for our long-term philosophical, social, and economic well-being depend too much on them.

# INDEX